KID
FAVORITES
MADE HEALTHY

Better Homes and Gardens® Books
Des Moines, Iowa

KID FAVORITES MADE HEALTHY

Editor: Jan Miller, R.D., L.D.
Contributing Editors: Tami Leonard;
   Martha Miller; Marcia K. Stanley, M.S., R.D.;
   Mary Williams
Senior Associate Design Director: Ken Carlson
Contributing Designer: Andrea Quam,
   Designgroup, Inc.
Copy Chief: Terri Fredrickson
Copy and Production Editor: Victoria Forlini
Editorial Operations Manager: Karen Schirm
Managers, Book Production: Pam Kvitne,
   Marjorie J. Schenkelberg, Rick von Holdt
Contributing Copy Editor: Karen Fraley
Contributing Proofreaders: Gretchen Kauffman,
   Susan J. Kling, Carolyn Peterson
Indexer: Elizabeth T. Parson
Editorial and Design Assistants: Karen McFadden, Mary Lee Gavin
Test Kitchen Director: Lynn Blanchard
Test Kitchen Product Supervisor: Jennifer Kalinowski, R.D.
Test Kitchen Home Economists: Marilyn Cornelius; Juliana Hale;
   Laura Harms, R.D.; Maryellyn Krantz; Jill Moberly; Dianna Nolin;
   Colleen Weeden; Lori Wilson; Charles Worthington

Meredith® Books
Editor in Chief: Linda Raglan Cunningham
Design Director: Matt Strelecki
Executive Editor, Food and Crafts: Jennifer Dorland Darling

Publisher: James D. Blume
Executive Director, Marketing: Jeffrey Myers
Executive Director, New Business Development: Todd M. Davis
Executive Director, Sales: Ken Zagor
Director, Operations: George A. Susral
Director, Production: Douglas M. Johnston
Business Director: Jim Leonard

Vice President and General Manager: Douglas J. Guendel

Better Homes and Gardens® Magazine
Editor in Chief: Karol DeWulf Nickell
Deputy Editor, Food and Entertaining: Nancy Hopkins

Meredith Publishing Group
President, Publishing Group: Stephen M. Lacy
Vice President-Publishing Director: Bob Mate

Meredith Corporation
Chairman and Chief Executive Officer: William T. Kerr

In Memoriam: E. T. Meredith III (1933–2003)

Our seal assures you that every recipe in *Kid Favorites Made Healthy* has been tested in the Better Homes and Gardens® Test Kitchen. This means that each recipe is practical and reliable, and meets our high standards of taste appeal. We guarantee your satisfaction with this book for as long as you own it.

All of us at Better Homes and Gardens® Books are dedicated to providing you with the information and ideas you need to create delicious foods. We welcome your comments and suggestions. Write to us at: Better Homes and Gardens Books, Cookbook Editorial Department, 1716 Locust St., Des Moines, IA 50309-3023.

If you would like to purchase any of our cooking, crafts, gardening, home improvement, or home decorating and design books, check wherever quality books are sold. Or visit us at: bhgbooks.com

HELP YOUR KIDS TO EAT SMART!

Do you have a child who won't go within 10 feet of a green vegetable? Or who complains when you try to limit high-calorie snacks and goodies? Let's face it, getting your kids to eat good-for-you food can be a major challenge. As a parent, it's no fun to be the food police!

Put away your food police badge! *Better Homes and Gardens® Kid Favorites Made Healthy* will ease the struggle around your dinner table. Written for parents of children ages 6 to 17*, it's filled with recipes your kids will love and you'll feel good about preparing. From classic kid-friendly main dishes such as Mighty Mac and Cheese and Crunchy Chicken Nuggets to healthful desserts—and everything in between—your kids won't suspect their new favorite dishes are loaded with nutrients.

In addition to irresistible recipes, you'll find a wealth of resources for keeping kids fit and healthy. If you are the parent of an overweight child, chances are your concerns may go beyond whether he or she is eating enough fruits and vegetables. You may be worrying about your child's self-esteem, the long-term health implications of the weight gain. You may not have the first idea about how to help your child lose weight. Read through "Ask the Experts" (pages 6-11) for sound advice for teaching your child to make better food choices, learn to become more active, and maintain a positive self-image.

If you, as a parent, are overweight, take this opportunity to partner with your child and work toward a healthier, more active, and fulfilling lifestyle. The research regarding parents as role models is overwhelmingly conclusive—actions speak louder than words for children and adolescents. You should encourage, support, and enable your kids to make the changes necessary for them to feel better and perform their best—but most importantly—you have to walk the talk. If your children see you eating more fruits and vegetables or putting on your tennis shoes to go walking, they may be more willing to try those things too.

Let *Better Homes and Gardens Kid Favorites Made Healthy* help you teach your children healthful lifelong eating habits. Whip up any one of these delicious recipes, shut off the television, and enjoy. Then—get moving! It's never too late to start.

*Consult your pediatrician about feeding your younger child.

According to **Dr. Nancy Krebs**, chairperson of the American Academy of Pediatrics Committee on Nutrition, 15 percent of U.S. children are overweight—that's almost 9 million children!

TABLE OF

YOU ARE WHAT YOU EAT.

So eat right from morning to night!

CONTENTS

Safari Dip, page 43

ASK THE EXPERTS

Pediatric Health

NANCY KREBS, M.D., M.S., R.D., *an associate professor of pediatrics at the University of Colorado School of Medicine, is also chairperson of the American Academy of Pediatrics Committee on Nutrition.*

Q. How do I know if my child is overweight?
A. For a parent, it's very difficult to make that call, and I wouldn't advise taking that job on yourself. As for adults, pediatricians use a Body Mass Index (BMI) to determine if a child or teenager (ages 2 to 20) is overweight, but it is plotted on age- and gender-specific growth charts. BMI is the measure of body fat based on height and weight.

Children tend to gain weight at a fairly steady rate through the middle years, with an increase in weight gain and growth during, and just prior to, puberty. Your child's calorie needs rise during times of rapid growth, gradually increasing as she moves through middle childhood into puberty. Don't become alarmed by this increase in weight. The growth charts account for this increase, and your pediatrician uses them to determine if the weight gain during this time is excessive.

Talk to your doctor about not where the child's BMI is now, but where is it trending. If the child is at the 85th percentile (which is right on the border of being at risk for being overweight) and a year from now she is still there, that's pretty good. But if in six months she's above the 90th percentile, that's not good.

Q. What are the health risks of having an overweight child?
A. If you are an overweight adolescent, there is an 80 percent chance you will stay overweight as an adult. More than 60 percent of overweight children between 5 and 10 years old already have at least one risk factor for cardiovascular disease. Other major health problems include diabetes and high blood pressure.

A 2001 study in *The Lancet* medical journal found that severely obese children already had stiff arteries, making them potentially susceptible to atherosclerosis as adults. These kids are at much higher risk to get these life-threatening diseases much earlier in life than kids who are not overweight. This could be the first generation in a century with a shorter life span than its parents.

Q. What is the best way for a child to lose weight safely without jeopardizing growth and development?
A. Some kids just need to grow into their weight, and it can happen at different times. Girls don't have much height growth after age 16, but boys can keep on growing throughout college. In general, for children, I recommend trying to lose one-half pound a week, but the first step is to maintain healthful eating habits and exercise. At our clinic, we teach families to learn new ways to eat. We tell kids to eat lots of fruits and vegetables every day, to eat sensible portion sizes, and to eat regularly. Teens often don't eat breakfast or lunch, and then they come home from school and eat until they go to bed. We also encourage families to limit the amount of times they eat at restaurants. The more families eat out, the more they place themselves in the danger zone of overeating.

Self-Esteem

JOHN P. FOREYT, PH.D., *is director of the Behavioral Medicine Research Center at Baylor College of Medicine in Houston. He is also a member of the National Institutes of Health's National Task Force on the Prevention and Treatment of Obesity and the American Obesity Association's Advisory Council.*

Q. If my child is overweight, how do I approach the topic without hurting self-esteem?
A. It sounds overly simple, but you just find a quiet time when you can sit down and talk about it. Of course, the parent has to be very sensitive, but the child knows he or she looks different from the other kids and may be relieved to be having the conversation. Talk in an understanding and empathetic way instead of laying down the law.

Older kids are more sensitive because of peer pressure, so parents need to tread lightly and really think about their words. A good way to start talking with older kids may be something like "I've been reading about the onset of diabetes and other weight-related problems in children, and I want to be sure you start life as healthfully as you can."

Q. What should I tell my child about responding to the cruel remarks or teasing from other children?
A. This is such a demeaning issue; obese and overweight kids suffer, ridicule and discrimination every day of their lives. It's very, very sad, especially for older kids.

The best way parents can counter this kind of cruelty is to build up the child's self-esteem every chance they get. At our center, we teach obese kids to be proud of themselves independently of their weight. Find things your kids are good at—a great sense of humor, a terrific reader or artist—and then strongly reinforce that. Always, always reinforce them. We were made in all shapes and sizes. We all can't be skinny, but we can all be healthy. Regular reinforcement of a child's self-esteem is one of the best things a parent can do.

Q. How can I help my child handle negative comments?
A. We teach children to respond by saying, "What you are saying hurts me, but I am working on it." By doing this, you are teaching your child to be aware of his or her feelings. I also remind the kids that if the insults don't stop, it's time to find new friends.

Q. What are the most important things a parent can do to help their overweight child?
A. DO NOT CRITICIZE. *Ever.* Find things they like doing to reinforce them, boost self-esteem, and be positive. Parents need to be good role models themselves and try to find ways to be active with their children. Give them healthful choices at mealtimes and make sure healthful foods are always on hand. Parents can start trying to do things on their own and move toward working with a professional if they find they need more help.

Also, eat dinner together as a family every night. It's a perfect chance to build self-esteem in children. By listening to what children have to say, parents send the message that what they do is important to them. Most adults and children eat more sensibly when they eat together, which helps manage weight better too.

SELF-ESTEEM BOOSTERS

1. In general, the more positive the parents' self-esteem, the more positive the child's will be. Be a good role model. Start by building your own self-esteem.

2. Find some way to praise your child every day. Make sure the praise is realistic and honest.

3. Focus on the positive aspects of your child's behavior. Even if you don't like some of the behavior, find something positive to focus on.

4. Put a picture of your child with family members next to your child's bed. This is a subtle reminder to your child that he/she has family support and is not alone in this world.

5. Communicate with your child. This means listening to how your child feels without making judgments about those feelings.

6. Keep criticism to a minimum. Criticism does not produce positive behavior. Praise does.

7. Teach your child to set goals, follow through, and complete projects. The projects can be small and short in the beginning and become more involved. This builds self-confidence and self-esteem and shows children they have some control in their lives.

8. Say "I love you" and mean it every day. Children need to hear it often, especially when it seems they don't deserve it.

9. Teach your child to say nice things and do good deeds. It builds good character and produces positive feelings within the child.

7

TOP TIPS FOR BEING A GOOD NUTRITION ROLE MODEL

1. Don't skip breakfast—it doesn't have to be a hot meal. Cereal and toast are still considered breakfast.

2. Allow your children to help with food selection and preparation; children as young as 4 can help choose appropriate items at the grocery store.

3. Turn off the television at meal times.

4. Don't pressure your children to clean their plates. There will be some foods they will dislike. Because children's taste buds change over time, keep reintroducing a variety of foods; they may eventually like something they initially refused.

5. Let your kids enjoy their favorite foods—there are no bad foods. Teach your children even sweets may be a part of a balanced diet.

6. Dine together as many times during the week as your schedule allows. Studies show kids who eat with their families tend to eat a wider variety of foods, have a better chance of meeting their nutritional needs, and are more likely to say no to drugs.

7. Drink your milk.

8. Snack on fresh fruits and vegetables more often than chips and processed foods.

9. Dine out cautiously—make wise choices when selecting your meal and watch the portion sizes. Limit your trips to fast-food restaurants.

Nutrition

SHEAH RARBACK, M.S., R.D., *is director of nutrition at the Mailman Center for Child Development at the University of Miami and spokesperson for the American Dietetic Association.*

Q. How do you determine appropriate portion sizes for children?
A. A young child's (ages 2 to 6) portion should be one-third to one-half of an adult portion. If you put too much food on young children's plates they won't eat anything—it's too much for them. Food's appearance impacts children. Serve a small portion and tell your children that if they still feel hunger, they can have more. If they don't feel hunger, they don't have to clean their plates. Portions for children ages 6 to 18 years are similar to those recommended for adults.

Q. What is the best resource for parents to use to determine portion sizes and adequate nutrition?
A. The U.S. Department of Agriculture created a Food Guide Pyramid for Young Children several years ago for kids 2 to 6 years old because most children are not eating the recommended numbers of servings from the five major food groups.

It's an adaptation of the Food Guide Pyramid for adults and is easier for kids to understand. (You can download a copy of the pyramid at www.usda.gov/cnpp.) For children older than 6, the Food Guide Pyramid is still an excellent basic guideline (page 9).

Q. How can I introduce "healthier" food into my picky eater's diet?
A. The first thing is for parents to set a good example. If you are not eating a variety of healthful foods, your kids aren't going to either. Make it a priority to have family meals several nights a week.

A recent study in the *Journal of Adolescent Health* (May 2003) shows that teenagers who ate three family meals a week ate more fruit, dairy, and vegetables than teens who ate less than three weekly family meals together. This just shows you the power of the parents as role models. These are adolescents, so imagine the impact this has on a 5-year-old child. The phrase "family meal" doesn't mean it has to be elaborate. Buy a rotisserie chicken at the grocery store, microwave frozen vegetables, and get quick-cooking brown rice. Frozen foods can be as tasty as fresh foods, and nutritionally they are just as good.

Eating together also teaches kids about food and manners. If you don't have family meals, your kids are going to learn their table manners in the school cafeteria.

Other tips:
* *Break out the dip. It's fun, tasty, and it helps kids eat more fruits and vegetables.*
* *Include your kids in the cooking process. Let them stir, measure, and pour things. Children are much more likely to taste something they helped make.*
* *Show your kids where the food comes from. Plan an outing to the local farmer's market or an apple orchard. Let your child help choose the foods you buy.*
* *Keep offering a variety of foods even if they turn them down. One day they will try something new and they may just like it.*

Q. We know low-calorie diets are not appropriate for overweight children because they may interfere with a child's normal growth and development. But if you correct portion sizes, aren't you reducing calories?

A. No. What you're doing is stopping food intake from being excessive. If you have a child who requires 1,600 calories a day and she is eating 1,800 calories, restricting the child's intake to 1,600 is not putting her on a diet. It's giving her the requirement she needs. You don't put a child on a diet. You create an eating plan that meets the child's growth needs. When obese children come to me for help, I often add foods because they are eating poorly and not making the right nutritional choices. They are eating a lot of empty calories.

Q. What can families do about the fast-food dilemma? How do you eat healthy on the run?

A. You can't avoid fast food. However, when I talk to people who are eating fast food three to four times a week, I tell them eating once a week at a fast-food place is enough. Then I give them alternatives so they make better choices.

For example, if you feel you must order french fries, split them among all the kids. Better yet, order a side salad instead. Don't go for mega sizes. Order milk instead of soda. Get the baked potato or order the smaller hamburger. If pizza is the menu item under consideration, a slice of vegetarian or cheese pizza is a better choice than sausage or pepperoni.

Food Guide Pyramid

A GUIDE TO DAILY FOOD CHOICES

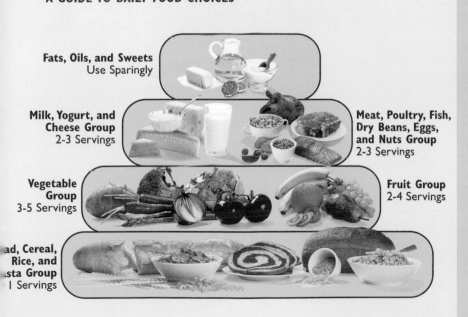

Fats, Oils, and Sweets
Use Sparingly

Milk, Yogurt, and Cheese Group
2-3 Servings

Meat, Poultry, Fish, Dry Beans, Eggs, and Nuts Group
2-3 Servings

Vegetable Group
3-5 Servings

Fruit Group
2-4 Servings

...ad, Cereal, Rice, and ...sta Group
... Servings

PYRAMID PORTIONS

Appropriate portions for children 6 to 18 years.

Bread, Cereal, Rice, and Pasta Group
* 1 slice of bread
* ½ cup cooked cereal, rice, or pasta
* 1 ounce of ready-to-eat cereal

Vegetable Group
* ½ cup cooked or raw vegetables
* 1 cup of raw leafy vegetables

Fruit Group
* 1 piece of fruit or melon wedge
* ¾ cup juice
* ½ cup canned fruit
* ¼ cup dried fruit

Milk Group
* 1 cup of milk or yogurt
* 2 ounces of cheese

Meat Group
* 2 to 3 ounces cooked, lean meat, poultry, or fish
* ½ cup cooked dry beans or ½ cup tofu or 1 egg counts as 1 ounce lean meat
* 2 tablespoons of peanut butter count as 1 ounce of meat

To teach your children normal portion size in a super-size world, give them a hand. The following guidelines will help determine how much food they are eating.

* palm (minus fingers) = 1 serving of meat, fish, or poultry
* tip of thumb to first joint = 1 tablespoon, 1 ounce of cheese
* tip of finger to first joint = 1 teaspoon
* clenched fist = 2 servings (1 cup) of potatoes, rice, or pasta
* cupped hand = 1 serving (½ cup) pasta, chopped fruit, or cooked veggies

TOP 10 FITNESS TIPS FOR PARENTS

1. Make exercise a part of your daily routine. Young eyes are watching.

2. Talk about the days you do exercise, not the days you miss.

3. Encourage activity your family can enjoy together—riding bikes, walking the dog, playing at a park, ice-skating, swimming.

4. Purchase gifts for the family that encourage activity—croquet, a basketball hoop, badminton, family passes to a fitness center.

5. Limit television viewing to 2 hours per day.

6. Take golf lessons or tennis lessons with your child—it's never too late to learn.

7. Turn up the music and dance with your kids.

8. Encourage participation, not performance, when trying new activities.

9. Build a birthday party around a physical activity—bowling, swimming, playing ball.

10. Support your child's desire to explore organized sports.

Physical Fitness

LYNN SWANN *is the chairman of the President's Council on Physical Fitness and Sports. In this role, he advises the president and the secretary of Health and Human Services about issues related to physical activity, fitness, and sports.*

Lynn Swann played wide receiver with the Pittsburgh Steelers, helping the team win four Super Bowls. Among his many awards, he was selected NFL Man of the Year in 1981, and in 2001 he was inducted into the Pro Football Hall of Fame. Swann also works as a sportscaster for ABC Sports and has been the national spokesperson for Big Brothers Big Sisters of America since 1980. He is the father of two slim boys who actually love to do sit-ups.

Q. What activities are appropriate for an overweight child?

A. First and foremost, any child or adult who has not been exercising regularly needs to check with a doctor prior to beginning an exercise program. You have to find out just where your child is healthwise so that whatever he does, he's moving in the right direction.

Second, talk to a fitness expert, if possible. Go to the local YMCA or Boys and Girls Clubs or just stop by a local health club to talk about your child beginning a workout program. These experts can give you a road map to follow.

The third and most important thing is to get started. It almost doesn't matter what your child does as long as he does something and does it consistently. Walk to school with your kids, buy them in-line skates, or take a hike every Saturday morning. Maybe your daughter or son can become a dog walker for neighborhood pets and pick up some extra money along the way.

Encourage your child to take up a sport. Many schools have eliminated sports programs because of lack of funding, so it's up to parents to help keep their children active. If you involve a kid in a game he enjoys, he gains physical benefits while engaging in something fun.

Q. How do you motivate children to increase their activity level?

A. Parents should exercise with their children. We are no longer a society where young people want only to listen to advice. They want the person giving the advice to follow it. Walk the walk. President Bush doesn't just pay lip service to physical activity; he pays sweat service. His activities—running and working out—are an integral part of his everyday life.

Introduce kids to a variety of sports. Perhaps they'll find a sport or several sports that they enjoy and will participate in for the long haul. The reason we focus on children is that if they understand the value of working out and being physically fit, these become priorities for the rest of their lives.

Q. How much exercise is enough?

A. The goal is to be physically active every day. Try to have children and teens consistently exercise up to one hour a day, five days a week. It would be wonderful if every child could do that.

Kids who are not exercising regularly now may not be able to be active for an hour. They may be able to handle 20 or 30 minutes of some type of exercise. It's important to remember that we are not trying to turn young kids into pro athletes. Kids who are interested in that direction are already intensely involved in sports. But even casually participating in sports can be the medicine that prevents your kids from getting diabetes, high blood pressure, and some forms of cancer.

Q. What are ideas for parents to help their kids increase activity?

A. If your kids enjoy riding a bike, make that a way they can consistently get exercise. Play basketball every night before dinner. Walking the dog is a good chore for kids and teenagers and happens to be a great form of exercise. In the fall, have your children rake instead of using a leaf blower. Perhaps they could do exercises at home. Herschel Walker, who played for the Dallas Cowboys and was a Heisman Trophy winner, was an incredibly strong player and always in great shape. He also was a world-class sprinter. He says he never lifted weights. However, when he watched TV, he would do sit-ups or push-ups every time a commercial came on for its entire length. Your kids can do the same thing. Perhaps they could run in place during the commercials. Just make moving a priority and you will notice a difference.

EXERCISE SAFETY

Exercising should be fun. No longer is it necessary to feel some pain in order to experience some gain. In fact, if your child hasn't been regularly exercising, take extra measures to ensure he or she is not overdoing it when he or she begins. Your child should be able to hold a conversation with you throughout an activity without struggling to catch his breath. Exercise should stop immediately if your child complains of any of the following symptoms:

* Pain
* Dizziness or faintness
* Nausea
* Severe fatigue

A few more things: If any activity your children choose requires protective gear, make sure they wear it at all times. Encourage your children to drink plenty of water before, during, and after any activity—even if they say they aren't thirsty—especially during warm weather.

11

For more information: President's Council on Physical Fitness and Sports HHH Building, Room 738 H 200 Independence Avenue, S.W. Washington, D.C. 20201 www.fitness.gov

"...If your kids enjoy riding a bike, make that a way they can consistently get exercise..."

RISE-AND-SHINE BREAKFASTS

Rouse your sleepyheads with these eye-opening breakfast favorites. Try a fast fruit smoothie, a hearty breakfast sandwich, or blueberry-studded pancakes to start the day with an energizing meal and smiling faces.

1

Corny Egg and Ham Sandwiches

Banana-Berry Smoothies

Just four ingredients and a quick whirl of the blender make a scrumptious breakfast that packs a healthful wallop.

Start to Finish: 10 minutes   Makes: 3 (about 8-ounce) servings

> 2 **ripe bananas, chilled**
> 1 **cup frozen unsweetened whole strawberries**
> 1 **8-ounce carton vanilla low-fat yogurt**
> ¾ **cup milk**
> **Fresh whole strawberries (optional)**

1. Cut bananas into chunks. In a blender container combine bananas, frozen strawberries, yogurt, and milk. Cover and blend until smooth. Pour into glasses or transfer to a small pitcher and chill up to 6 hours. If desired, garnish with whole strawberries.

Nutrition Facts per serving: 182 cal., 3 g total fat (1 g sat. fat), 9 mg chol., 82 mg sodium, 35 g carbo., 3 g fiber, 7 g pro.
Daily Values: 5% vit. A, 59% vit. C, 22% calcium, 3% iron
Exchanges: ½ Milk, 1½ Fruit

Tango Mango Smoothies

Breakfast at home doesn't have to be labor-intensive. This tasty smoothie is as easy as it is nutritious.

Start to Finish: 10 minutes   Makes: 6 (6-ounce) servings

> 2 **ripe bananas, chilled**
> ⅔ **cup peeled mango slices**
> 1 **12-ounce can mango, peach, apricot, or other fruit nectar, chilled**
> 1 **cup plain fat-free yogurt**
> 1 **tablespoon honey (optional)**
> **Cut-up fresh fruit such as bananas, peeled kiwifruit, and/or peeled mango (optional)**

1. Cut bananas into chunks. In a blender container combine bananas, mango, fruit nectar, yogurt, and, if desired, honey. Cover and blend until smooth. Pour into six chilled glasses. If desired, garnish with cut-up fresh fruit.

Nutrition Facts per serving: 108 cal., 0 g total fat (0 g sat. fat), 1 mg chol., 33 mg sodium, 24 g carbo., 1 g fiber, 3 g pro.
Daily Values: 15% vit. A, 27% vit. C, 9% calcium, 1% iron
Exchanges: ½ Milk, 1 Fruit

Wake-Up Cocoa Mix

Rise, shine, and serve this sure-to-please cocoa. Your children won't know that this chocolate delight contains fat-free milk.

Start to Finish: 10 minutes   *Makes:* 4⅓ cups mix (13 servings)

1¾ **cups nonfat dry milk powder**
1 **cup sifted powdered sugar**
½ **cup powdered fat-free nondairy creamer**
⅓ **cup sifted unsweetened cocoa powder**
2 **cups miniature marshmallows**
Miniature marshmallows (optional)

1. For mix, in a medium bowl combine dry milk powder, powdered sugar, nondairy creamer, and cocoa powder. Stir in the 2 cups marshmallows. Store in an airtight container at room temperature for up to 3 months.

2. For each serving, place ⅓ cup of the cocoa mix in a cup. Add ¾ cup boiling water. Stir well. If desired, top with additional miniature marshmallows.

Nutrition Facts per serving: 165 cal., 3 g total fat (1 g sat. fat), 3 mg chol., 68 mg sodium, 30 g carbo., 0 g fiber, 4 g pro.
Daily Values: 4% vit. A, 1% vit. C, 16% calcium, 2% iron.
Exchanges: 1 Other Carbo., ½ Milk

Peppermint Cocoa: Prepare mix as directed. For each serving, place ⅓ cup of the cocoa mix and 1½ teaspoons finely crushed peppermint candy in a cup. Add ¾ cup boiling water. Stir well. If desired, top with additional miniature marshmallows and finely crushed peppermint candy.

Smiling Baked Oatmeal

This tasty oatmeal casserole puts a smile on your kids' faces and gives you the comfort of knowing that you started their day with a healthy serving of protein and soluble fiber.

Prep: 10 minutes *Bake:* 30 minutes *Oven:* 350°F *Makes:* 4 servings

Nonstick cooking spray
1 **cup quick-cooking rolled oats**
½ **cup mixed dried fruit bits**
2 **cups fat-free milk**
¼ **cup refrigerated or frozen egg product, thawed**
¼ **cup sugar**
½ **teaspoon vanilla**
⅛ **teaspoon salt**
Mixed dried fruit bits and/or cut-up maraschino cherries
2 **tablespoons light pancake and waffle syrup product (optional)**

1. Lightly coat four 10-ounce custard cups with cooking spray; set aside. Stir together the oats and the ½ cup fruit bits. Divide oat mixture among the four custard cups. In a medium bowl combine milk, egg product, sugar, vanilla, and salt, stirring to dissolve sugar and salt. Pour milk mixture into the custard cups, dividing evenly. Place custard cups in a shallow baking pan.

2. Bake in a 350° oven for 30 to 35 minutes or until centers are nearly set. Arrange additional dried fruit bits on top of each serving to make a smiling face. Serve warm. If desired, drizzle with syrup.

16

Nutrition Facts per serving: 243 cal., 2 g total fat (0 g sat. fat), 2 mg chol., 175 mg sodium, 48 g carbo., 2 g fiber, 10 g pro.
Daily Values: 6% vit. A, 3% vit. C, 17% calcium, 8% iron
Exchanges: ½ Milk, 1½ Fruit, 1½ Starch

I'm Full! Up to the age of 5, kids have an excellent built-in regulator that tells them when they have eaten just enough. Children older than 5 years start to ignore their body's satiety mechanism. They're more tempted to eat food just because it's there or to combat boredom. Teach your kids how to recognize when they're truly hungry and talk to them about alternate activities to help beat the boredom blues.

Granny's Granola

Just a half cup in the morning provides your kids carbohydrates for energy and protein to keep them going until lunchtime. Serve it over low-fat yogurt for an added calcium kick.

Prep: 12 minutes   Bake: 45 minutes
Cool: 30 minutes   Oven: 325°F
Makes: 8 (½-cup) servings

Nonstick cooking spray
3 cups regular rolled oats
1 cup coarsely shredded unpeeled apple
½ cup toasted wheat germ
¼ cup water
¼ cup honey
1½ teaspoons ground cinnamon
1 teaspoon vanilla or ½ teaspoon almond extract
Milk
Fresh raspberries, blueberries, and/or sliced strawberries (optional)

1. Lightly coat a 15×10×1-inch baking pan with cooking spray; set aside. In a large bowl combine oats, apple, and wheat germ; mix well. In a small saucepan stir together water, honey, and cinnamon. Bring to boiling; remove from heat. Stir in vanilla. Pour over the oat mixture; toss to coat. Spread oat mixture evenly in prepared baking pan.

2. Bake in a 325° oven about 45 minutes or until golden brown, stirring occasionally. Spread granola onto foil. Cool about 30 minutes before serving. Serve the granola with milk and, if desired, fresh berries. Store remaining granola in a tightly covered container in the refrigerator up to 2 weeks.

Nutrition Facts per serving: 272 cal., 6 g total fat (2 g sat. fat), 10 mg chol., 63 mg sodium, 45 g carbo., 5 g fiber, 11 g pro.
Daily Values: 5% vit. A, 4% vit. C, 18% calcium, 14% iron
Exchanges: ½ Milk, 2½ Starch, ½ Fat

18

Bunch of Banana Bread

Pair this cinnamon-spiked sweet bread with a low-fat scrambled egg for a burst of protein.

Prep: 15 minutes   Bake: 45 minutes   Oven: 350°F   Makes: 1 loaf (16 servings)

Nonstick cooking spray
1½ cups all-purpose flour
1¼ teaspoons baking powder
½ teaspoon baking soda
½ teaspoon ground cinnamon
⅛ teaspoon salt
2 slightly beaten egg whites
1 cup mashed banana (3 medium)
¾ cup sugar
¼ cup cooking oil

1. Lightly coat an 8×4×2-inch loaf pan with cooking spray; set aside. In a medium bowl combine flour, baking powder, baking soda, cinnamon, and salt. Set aside.

2. In a large bowl stir together the egg whites, banana, sugar, and oil. Add flour mixture all at once to banana mixture. Stir just until moistened (the batter should be lumpy). Spoon batter into prepared pan.

3. Bake in a 350° oven for 45 to 50 minutes or until a wooden toothpick inserted near the center comes out clean.

4. Cool in pan on a wire rack for 10 minutes. Remove from pan. Cool completely on rack. Wrap and store overnight before slicing.

Nutrition Facts per serving: 127 cal., 4 g total fat (1 g sat. fat), 0 mg chol., 96 mg sodium, 23 g carbo., 1 g fiber, 2 g pro.
Daily Values: 3% vit. C, 2% calcium, 3% iron
Exchanges: 1 Starch, ½ Other Carbo., ½ Fat

Sunrise Biscuits

Orange-laced cream cheese complements these savory biscuits. They're great for breakfast, or pack them with hot soup for a lunchtime treat.

Prep: 20 minutes   Bake: 10 minutes   Oven: 450°F   Makes: 10 biscuits

2 cups all-purpose flour
2 teaspoons baking powder
¼ teaspoon salt
⅓ cup butter or margarine
¾ cup buttermilk
1 recipe Orange Spread (optional)

1. In a medium bowl combine flour, baking powder, and salt. Using a pastry blender, cut in the butter until mixture resembles coarse crumbs. Make a well in the center of the flour mixture. Add buttermilk all at once. Using a fork, stir just until moistened.

2. Turn dough out onto a lightly floured surface. Knead dough by folding and gently pressing dough for 4 to 6 strokes or just until dough holds together. Pat or lightly roll dough to ½-inch thickness. Cut with a 2-inch biscuit cutter, dipping cutter into flour between cuts. Place biscuits on an ungreased baking sheet.

3. Bake in a 450° oven for 10 to 12 minutes or until golden. Serve warm. If desired, serve with Orange Spread.

Nutrition Facts per biscuit: 155 cal., 7 g total fat (4 g sat. fat), 18 mg chol., 223 mg sodium, 20 g carbo., 1 g fiber, 3 g pro.
Daily Values: 5% vit. A, 8% calcium, 7% iron
Exchanges: 1½ Starch, 1 Fat

Orange Spread: In a small bowl stir together half of an 8-ounce package reduced-fat cream cheese (Neufchâtel), softened, and 2 tablespoons orange marmalade or peach or apricot preserves until smooth. Makes about ½ cup.

Morning Glory Muffins

Kick off the day with warm muffins studded with carrots, apples, raisins, and pineapple.

Prep: *30 minutes*   Bake: *18 minutes*
Oven: *375°F*   Makes: *18 muffins*

- 2 **cups all-purpose flour**
- 2 **teaspoons baking soda**
- 2 **teaspoons ground cinnamon**
- ½ **teaspoon salt**
- 1¼ **cups packed brown sugar**
- 2 **medium apples, peeled, cored, and chopped (1⅓ cups)**
- 1¼ **cups finely shredded carrots**
- ½ **cup raisins**
- 1 **8-ounce can crushed pineapple (juice pack), undrained**
- ⅔ **cup cooking oil**
- 3 **eggs**
- ½ **teaspoon vanilla**

1. Line eighteen 2½-inch muffin cups with paper bake cups; set aside.

2. In a large bowl combine flour, baking soda, cinnamon, and salt; stir in brown sugar. Stir in apples, carrots, and raisins. In a medium bowl combine undrained pineapple, oil, eggs, and vanilla. Add pineapple mixture to flour mixture; stir just until moistened.

3. Spoon batter into prepared muffin cups. Bake in a 375° oven about 18 minutes or until a wooden toothpick inserted in centers comes out clean. Cool in muffin cups on wire rack for 5 minutes. Remove from muffin cups; serve warm.

Nutrition Facts per muffin: 221 cal., 9 g total fat (1 g sat. fat), 35 mg chol., 225 mg sodium, 33 g carbo., 1 g fiber, 3 g pro.
Daily Values: 44% vit. A, 4% vit. C, 3% calcium, 8% iron
Exchanges: 1 Fruit, 1 Starch, 2 Fat

Peanut Butter Breakfast Sandwiches

Can't get the kids to eat in the morning? They'll anxiously wait for breakfast when you serve toasted French bread stuffed with peanut butter, honey, and banana.

Start to Finish: 30 minutes   Makes: 8 servings

- ½ **cup reduced-fat or regular peanut butter**
- 8 **½-inch slices French bread**
- 2 **tablespoons honey**
- 2 **medium bananas**
- 2 **beaten eggs**
- ½ **cup milk**
- ¼ **teaspoon ground cinnamon**
- 1 **tablespoon butter or margarine**
- ½ **cup fruit preserves or jam (any flavor)**

1. Spread peanut butter evenly onto one side of each slice of bread. Drizzle honey over the peanut butter. Cut each banana in half lengthwise and then cut in half crosswise (8 pieces total). Arrange 2 banana pieces on 4 of the prepared bread slices. Top with remaining bread slices, peanut butter sides down.

2. In a shallow bowl combine eggs, milk, and cinnamon. Carefully dip sandwiches into egg mixture, coating both sides.

3. Melt butter in a large skillet or on a large griddle over medium heat. Cook sandwiches in hot butter about 2 minutes on each side or until golden.

4. Meanwhile, in a small saucepan heat fruit preserves over medium-low heat until melted, stirring frequently. To serve, cut warm sandwiches in half crosswise. Drizzle with warm fruit preserves.

Nutrition Facts per serving: 302 cal., 10 g total fat (3 g sat. fat), 58 mg chol., 323 mg sodium, 46 g carbo., 3 g fiber, 9 g pro.
Daily Values: 4% vit. A, 8% vit. C, 6% calcium, 8% iron
Exchanges: 1 Fruit, 2 Starch, ½ Medium-Fat Meat, 1 Fat

Corny Egg and Ham Sandwiches

Kids will love these open-face sandwiches that taste like ones from a fast-food restaurant. You'll know that the healthful sandwiches feature less fat and more nutrients than their fast-food counterparts.

Start to Finish: 30 minutes   *Makes:* 4 servings

Nonstick cooking spray
4 beaten eggs
¼ cup milk
¼ teaspoon salt
⅛ teaspoon black pepper
½ cup chopped cooked ham
⅓ cup frozen whole kernel corn, thawed
4 English muffins, halved and toasted
4 slices reduced-fat American cheese, halved

1. Lightly coat a medium skillet with cooking spray. Heat skillet over medium heat. In a small bowl beat together eggs, milk, salt, and pepper. Add to skillet. Cook, without stirring, until egg mixture begins to set on the bottom and around the edge. Using a spatula, lift and fold the partially cooked egg mixture so uncooked portion flows underneath. Continue cooking and folding until egg mixture is cooked through but still glossy and moist. Remove from heat. Stir in the ham and corn.

2. Place 4 English muffin halves on a baking sheet. Top each with a half slice of cheese, then top with some of the egg mixture. Add remaining cheese slices. Broil 4 to 5 inches from the heat for 1 to 2 minutes or until the cheese melts. Top with remaining muffin halves. Serve immediately.

Nutrition Facts per serving: 297 cal., 11 g total fat (4 g sat. fat), 233 mg chol., 951 mg sodium, 31 g carbo., 2 g fiber, 18 g pro.
Daily Values: 13% vit. A, 2% vit. C, 34% calcium, 13% iron
Exchanges: 2 Starch, 2 Medium-Fat Meat

24

Tex-Mex Breakfast Pizza

It's a kid's dream come true—pizza for breakfast. This nourishing version features hash brown potatoes, tomatoes, scrambled eggs, and reduced-fat cheese.

Prep: 25 minutes   Bake: 8 minutes   Oven: 375°F   Makes: 8 servings

    Nonstick cooking spray
1½ cups frozen loose-pack diced hash brown potatoes, thawed
¼ cup sliced green onions (2)
1 to 2 canned whole green chile peppers, drained, seeded, and chopped
¼ teaspoon ground cumin
1 clove garlic, minced
1 cup refrigerated or frozen egg product, thawed
¼ cup milk
1 tablespoon snipped fresh cilantro
1 16-ounce Italian bread shell (Boboli)
½ cup shredded reduced-fat Monterey Jack cheese (2 ounces)
1 small tomato, seeded and chopped

1. Lightly coat a large skillet with cooking spray. Heat over medium heat. Add the potatoes, green onions, chile peppers, cumin, and garlic. Cook and stir about 3 minutes or until the vegetables are tender.

2. In a small bowl beat together egg product, milk, and cilantro; add to potato mixture in skillet. Cook, without stirring, until mixture begins to set on the bottom and around the edge. Using a spatula, lift and fold the partially cooked mixture so uncooked portion flows underneath. Continue cooking and folding until mixture is cooked through but still glossy and moist. Remove from heat.

3. To assemble pizza, place the bread shell on a large baking sheet or a 12-inch pizza pan. Sprinkle half of the cheese over the shell. Top with egg mixture, tomato, and the remaining cheese.

4. Bake in a 375° oven for 8 to 10 minutes or until cheese is melted.

Nutrition Facts per serving: 227 cal., 5 g total fat (1 g sat. fat), 8 mg chol., 429 mg sodium, 33 g carbo., 2 g fiber, 13 g pro.
Daily Values: 4% vit. A, 13% vit. C, 14% calcium, 12% iron
Exchanges: ½ Vegetable, 2 Starch, 1 Lean Meat

Turkey-Apple Sausage Patties

Sausage lovers appreciate the spiciness of these low-fat patties made with bits of apple and snipped fresh sage.

Prep: 15 minutes   Broil: 10 minutes   Makes: 4 servings

½ **cup shredded, peeled apple**

2 **tablespoons soft bread crumbs**

1½ **teaspoons snipped fresh sage or ½ teaspoon dried sage, crushed**

¼ **teaspoon black pepper**

⅛ **teaspoon salt**

⅛ **teaspoon paprika**

⅛ **teaspoon cayenne pepper**

Dash ground nutmeg

8 **ounces uncooked ground turkey**

Nonstick cooking spray

1. In a large bowl combine the shredded apple, bread crumbs, sage, black pepper, salt, paprika, cayenne pepper, and nutmeg. Add the turkey; mix well. Shape mixture into four ½-inch-thick patties.

2. Lightly coat the unheated rack of a broiler pan with cooking spray. Arrange patties on rack. Broil 4 to 5 inches from the heat about 10 minutes or until no longer pink (165°F), turning once. Or coat a large skillet with cooking spray. Heat over medium heat. Add sausage and cook for 8 to 10 minutes or until no longer pink (165°F), turning once.

Nutrition Facts per serving: 98 cal., 5 g total fat (1 g sat. fat), 45 mg chol., 120 mg sodium, 3 g carbo., 0 g fiber, 10 g pro.
Daily Values: 2% vit. A, 2% vit. C, 1% calcium, 4% iron
Exchanges: 1½ Lean Meat

26

Breakfast—Don't skip it!

Kids who eat breakfast are more likely to stay alert in school throughout the day, keep their weight under control, meet their daily nutrient requirements, have lower blood cholesterol levels, and achieve better overall school attendance. And if you're looking for a little more family togetherness, breakfast is the perfect time to sit down to review schedules, share advice, and lend encouragement if a stressful day lies ahead.

Blueberry Pancakes

Serve these lively, orange-sauced and blueberry-packed pancakes for a smart start in the morning.

Prep: 20 minutes   Cook: 4 minutes per batch   Makes: 4 to 5 servings (2 pancakes and 2 tablespoons sauce per serving)

- 1 **cup all-purpose flour**
- 1 **tablespoon sugar**
- 1 **teaspoon baking powder**
- ½ **teaspoon baking soda**
- ⅛ **teaspoon salt**
- 1 **slightly beaten egg white**
- 1 **cup buttermilk**
- 2 **teaspoons cooking oil**
- 1 **teaspoon vanilla**
- ¾ **cup fresh or frozen blueberries**
- **Nonstick cooking spray**
- 1 **recipe Orange Sauce**
- **Orange wedges and/or fresh blueberries (optional)**

1. In a medium bowl stir together flour, sugar, baking powder, baking soda, and salt.

2. In another bowl stir together the egg white, buttermilk, cooking oil, and vanilla. Add all at once to the flour mixture. Stir just until moistened (batter should be lumpy). Gently fold in blueberries.

3. Lightly coat a nonstick griddle or heavy skillet with cooking spray. Heat over medium heat. For each pancake, pour about ¼ cup of the batter onto hot griddle. Cook about 2 minutes on each side or until pancakes are golden brown, turning to second sides when pancakes have bubbly surfaces and edges are slightly dry. Serve with Orange Sauce. If desired, garnish with orange wedges and/or additional blueberries. Cover and chill any remaining Orange Sauce.

Orange Sauce: In a small saucepan stir together ¼ cup thawed, frozen orange juice concentrate; 1 tablespoon sugar; and 1 tablespoon cornstarch. Stir in 1 cup water. Cook and stir over medium heat until thickened and bubbly. Cook and stir for 2 minutes more. Serve warm with pancakes.

Nutrition Facts per serving: 230 cal., 3 g total fat (1 g sat. fat), 2 mg chol., 413 mg sodium, 43 g carbo., 2 g fiber, 6 g pro.
Daily Values: 2% vit. A, 51% vit. C, 14% calcium, 8% iron
Exchanges: 1 Fruit, 2 Starch

Crunch-Topped French Toast

Perfect for the morning after slumber parties—this make-ahead breakfast entrée is baked with a crunchy topping and sweetened with fresh strawberries.

Prep: 20 minutes   Chill: 2 to 24 hours
Bake: 30 minutes   Oven: 375°F   Makes: 6 servings

    Nonstick cooking spray

1 **cup evaporated fat-free milk**

¾ **cup refrigerated or frozen egg product, thawed, or**
   3 slightly beaten eggs

3 **tablespoons sugar**

2 **teaspoons vanilla**

½ **teaspoon ground cinnamon**

¼ **teaspoon ground nutmeg**

6 **1-inch slices Italian bread (3 to 4 inches in diameter)**

1 **large shredded wheat biscuit, crushed (²⁄₃ cup)**

1 **tablespoon butter or margarine, melted**

2 **cups sliced strawberries**

3 **tablespoons sugar**

½ **teaspoon ground cinnamon**

1. Lightly coat a 2-quart rectangular baking dish with cooking spray; set aside. In a medium bowl beat together the evaporated milk, egg product, 3 tablespoons sugar, vanilla, ½ teaspoon cinnamon, and nutmeg. Arrange the bread slices in a single layer in prepared baking dish. Pour egg product mixture evenly over slices. Cover and chill for 2 to 24 hours, turning bread slices once with a wide spatula.

2. Combine crushed shredded wheat biscuit and melted butter; sprinkle evenly over the bread slices. Bake, uncovered, in a 375° oven about 30 minutes or until light brown.

3. Meanwhile, in a small bowl toss together strawberries, 3 tablespoons sugar, and ½ teaspoon cinnamon. Serve with French toast.

28

Nutrition Facts per serving: 227 cal., 3 g total fat (2 g sat. fat), 7 mg chol., 296 mg sodium, 39 g carbo., 3 g fiber, 10 g pro.
Daily Values: 7% vit. A, 46% vit. C, 17% calcium, 11% iron
Exchanges: ½ Fruit, 2 Starch, ½ Lean Meat

Peter Pumpkin Pancakes

These pancakes taste like pumpkin pie for breakfast—perfect for a weekend family brunch. Kids of all ages won't suspect they're getting healthy doses of vitamins A and C.

Prep: 20 minutes   Cook: 4 minutes per batch   Makes: 8 servings

- 2 cups all-purpose flour
- 2 tablespoons packed brown sugar
- 1 tablespoon baking powder
- ½ teaspoon salt
- ½ teaspoon pumpkin pie spice
- 1½ cups fat-free milk
- 1 cup canned pumpkin
- ½ cup refrigerated or frozen egg product, thawed
- 2 tablespoons cooking oil
- Nonstick cooking spray
- 1 recipe **Orange Syrup**
- 1 orange, peeled and sectioned (optional)

1. In a medium bowl stir together flour, brown sugar, baking powder, salt, and pumpkin pie spice.

2. In another medium bowl combine the milk, pumpkin, egg product, and oil. Add the milk mixture all at once to flour mixture. Stir just until moistened (batter should be lumpy).

3. Lightly coat a nonstick griddle or heavy skillet with cooking spray. Heat over medium heat. For each pancake, pour about ¼ cup batter onto the hot griddle or skillet. Cook over medium heat about 2 minutes on each side or until pancakes are golden brown, turning to second sides when pancakes have bubbly surfaces and edges are slightly dry. Serve warm with Orange Syrup and, if desired, orange sections.

Orange Syrup: In a small saucepan stir together 1 cup orange juice, 2 tablespoons honey, 2½ teaspoons cornstarch, and ¼ teaspoon ground cinnamon. Cook and stir over medium heat until thickened and bubbly. Cook and stir for 2 minutes more. Serve warm with pancakes. Makes about 1 cup.

Nutrition Facts per serving: 220 cal., 4 g total fat (1 g sat. fat), 1 mg chol., 348 mg sodium, 39 g carbo., 2 g fiber, 7 g pro.
Daily Values: 139% vit. A, 29% vit. C, 17% calcium, 13% iron
Exchanges: 2½ Starch, ½ Fat

Fruit-Filled Puffs

Skipping breakfast puts your metabolism in slow gear. Begin the day right with individual puffy pancakes filled with fresh fruit.

Prep: 10 minutes   Bake: 25 minutes   Stand: 5 minutes   Oven: 400°F   Makes: 4 servings

> **Nonstick cooking spray**
>
> ½ **cup refrigerated or frozen egg product, thawed, or**
> **1 whole egg plus 1 egg white**
>
> ¼ **cup all-purpose flour**
>
> ¼ **cup fat-free milk**
>
> 1 **tablespoon cooking oil**
>
> ¼ **teaspoon salt**
>
> 2 **cups fresh fruit (such as peeled and sliced kiwifruit, raspberries,**
> **blackberries, blueberries, sliced bananas, sliced strawberries, seedless**
> **grapes, peeled and sliced peaches, sliced nectarines, sliced apricots,**
> **and/or pitted and halved sweet cherries)**
>
> 2 **tablespoons orange marmalade, warmed**

1. Lightly coat four 4¼-inch pie plates or 4½-inch foil tart pans with cooking spray. Set aside.

2. In a large bowl use a rotary beater or whisk to beat together egg product, flour, milk, oil, and salt until smooth. Divide batter among prepared pans.

3. Bake in a 400° oven about 25 minutes or until brown and puffy. Turn off oven; let stand in oven 5 minutes. Remove from oven; immediately transfer pancakes to 4 bowls. Spoon some of the fruit into center of each pancake. Drizzle fruit with warmed orange marmalade.

Nutrition Facts per serving: 148 cal., 4 g total fat (1 g sat. fat), 0 mg chol., 204 mg sodium, 24 g carbo., 2 g fiber, 5 g pro.
Daily Values: 4% vit. A, 44% vit. C, 4% calcium, 7% iron
Exchanges: 1 Fruit, ½ Starch, ½ Very Lean Meat, ½ Fat

Apple Surprise Rolls

Don't tell! The surprise in these sweet, low-fat breakfast pastries is the apple and fruit filling hidden in the center of each roll.

Prep: 45 minutes   Rise: 30 minutes   Bake: 12 minutes   Oven: 375°F   Makes: 16 rolls

    1 16-ounce package hot roll mix
    1 medium cooking apple, finely chopped (1 cup)
    ¼ cup mixed dried fruit bits or raisins
    2 tablespoons packed brown sugar
    ½ teaspoon ground cinnamon
      Nonstick cooking spray
    ½ cup sifted powdered sugar
    1½ to 2 teaspoons milk

1. Prepare hot roll mix according to package directions. Knead the dough; allow to rest as directed. Meanwhile, for filling, in a small bowl stir together apple, dried fruit bits, brown sugar, and cinnamon. Lightly coat 2 baking sheets with cooking spray; set aside.

2. Divide dough into 16 pieces. Flatten each piece into a 3-inch circle. Spoon 1 rounded teaspoon of filling onto each circle. Shape the dough around the filling to enclose, pulling dough until smooth and rounded. Place, rounded sides up, on greased baking sheets. Cover and let rise in a warm place until nearly double in size (about 30 minutes).

3. Bake in a 375° oven for 12 to 15 minutes or until golden. Cool slightly on a wire rack. For icing, in a small bowl stir together powdered sugar and enough milk to make of drizzling consistency. Drizzle over rolls.

Nutrition Facts per roll: 149 cal., 2 g total fat (0 g sat. fat), 13 mg chol., 187 mg sodium, 29 g carbo., 0 g fiber, 4 g pro.
Daily Values: 1% vit. C, 5% iron
Exchanges: 1 Fruit, 1 Starch

32

Raspberry and Cream Cheese Cake

The cheesecake-like topping and fresh raspberries make this low-fat coffee cake better than good—it's sensational!

Prep: *20 minutes* Bake: *30 minutes*
Oven: *375°F* Makes: *10 servings*

Nonstick cooking spray

1¼ **cups all-purpose flour**

1¼ **teaspoons baking powder**

1 **teaspoon finely shredded lemon or orange peel**

¼ **teaspoon baking soda**

1 **cup granulated sugar**

3 **tablespoons butter or margarine, softened**

¼ **cup refrigerated or frozen egg product, thawed**

1 **teaspoon vanilla**

½ **cup buttermilk**

2 **ounces reduced-fat cream cheese (Neufchâtel), softened**

2 **tablespoons refrigerated or frozen egg product, thawed**

1 **cup raspberries or thinly sliced apricots or nectarines**

Sifted powdered sugar (optional)

1. Lightly coat a 9×1½-inch round baking pan with cooking spray; set aside. Stir together flour, baking powder, lemon peel, soda, and ¼ teaspoon salt; set aside. In a mixing bowl beat ¾ cup of granulated sugar and butter with an electric mixer on medium to high speed until combined. Add the ¼ cup egg product and the vanilla. Beat on low to medium speed for 1 minute. Alternately add the flour mixture and buttermilk, beating just until combined after each addition. Pour into prepared pan.

2. In a small mixing bowl beat the cream cheese and the remaining ¼ cup granulated sugar on medium to high speed until combined. Add the 2 tablespoons egg product. Beat well. Arrange raspberries over the batter. Pour the cream cheese mixture over all.

3. Bake in a 375° oven for 30 to 35 minutes or until a wooden toothpick inserted near center comes out clean. Cool slightly on wire rack. Serve warm. If desired, top with additional fruit and sprinkle with sifted powdered sugar.

Nutrition Facts per serving: 193 cal., 5 g total fat (3 g sat. fat), 15 mg chol., 228 mg sodium, 33 g carbo., 1 g fiber, 4 g pro.
Daily Values: 5% vit. A, 6% vit. C, 6% calcium, 5% iron
Exchanges: 1 Starch, 1 Other Carbo., 1 Fat

GRAB-AND-GO SNACKS

Need an after-school snack? Or just a little morsel to help your youngsters make it to mealtime? From Double Dippin' Fruit to Mango Magic Pops, kids will love these tasty treats, and you'll feel good knowing they're deliciously nutritious.

2

Yam and Jam Muffins

Oat and Nut Crunch Mix

Satisfy the young snack monsters in your home with this sweetly spiced mix made from oat cereal, almonds, and dried cherries.

Prep: 10 minutes   Bake: 20 minutes   Cool: 30 minutes
Oven: 300°F   Makes: 20 servings (5 cups)

- 4 **cups sweetened oat square cereal or brown sugar-flavored oat biscuit cereal**
- ½ **cup sliced almonds**
- 2 **tablespoons butter or margarine, melted**
- ½ **teaspoon apple pie spice**
- **Dash salt**
- 1 **cup dried cherries and/or light raisins**

1. In a 15×10×1-inch baking pan combine cereal and almonds. In a small bowl stir together melted butter, apple pie spice, and salt. Drizzle butter mixture over cereal mixture; toss to coat.

2. Bake in a 300° oven about 20 minutes or until almonds are toasted, stirring once during baking. Cool in pan on a wire rack for 20 minutes. Stir in dried cherries. Cool completely. Store in a tightly covered container at room temperature up to 1 week.

Nutrition Facts per serving: 83 cal., 3 g total fat (1 g sat. fat), 3 mg chol., 63 mg sodium, 12 g carbo., 1 g fiber, 2 g pro.
Daily Values: 1% vit. A, 3% calcium, 14% iron
Exchanges: 1 Starch

Cheesy Chili Popcorn

Do your kids love salty snacks? Give them this chili- and cheese-spiced popcorn. It's low in fat and calories and high in flavor.

Start to Finish: 10 minutes   *Makes:* 10 servings (about 8 cups)

- **8 cups popped popcorn**
- **2 tablespoons butter or margarine, melted**
- **1 teaspoon chili powder**
- **⅛ teaspoon garlic powder**
- **2 tablespoons grated Parmesan cheese**

1. Place popcorn in a large bowl. In a small bowl stir together butter, chili powder, and garlic powder. Drizzle over popcorn; toss to coat. Sprinkle with Parmesan cheese; toss to coat. Store in a tightly covered container at room temperature up to 3 days.

Nutrition Facts per serving: 51 cal., 3 g total fat (2 g sat. fat), 7 mg chol., 46 mg sodium, 5 g carbo., 1 g fiber, 1 g pro.
Daily Values: 4% vit. A, 2% calcium, 1% iron
Exchanges: ½ Starch, ½ Fat

Peanut-Packed Munch Mix

Fiber-packed shredded wheat biscuit cereal takes on kid-pleasing proportions when it's baked with peanuts and peanut butter.

Prep: 10 minutes   Bake: 10 minutes   Cool: 30 minutes
Oven: 350°F   Makes: 14 servings (7 cups)

- **5 cups bite-size shredded wheat biscuits**
- **1 cup unsalted peanuts**
- **¼ cup creamy peanut butter**
- **2 tablespoons butter or margarine**
- **1 tablespoon honey**
- **½ cup mixed dried fruit bits or raisins**

1. In a 13×9×2-inch baking pan combine shredded wheat biscuits and peanuts. Set aside.

2. In a small saucepan cook and stir peanut butter, butter, and honey over low heat until mixture is melted. Drizzle over cereal mixture, tossing to coat.

3. Bake in a 350° oven for 10 minutes, stirring twice during baking. Cool in pan on a wire rack about 10 minutes. Stir in mixed dried fruit bits. Cool completely. Store in a tightly covered container at room temperature up to 1 week.

Nutrition Facts per serving: 181 cal., 10 g total fat (2 g sat. fat), 5 mg chol., 42 mg sodium, 22 g carbo., 2 g fiber, 6 g pro.
Daily Values: 1% vit. A, 1% calcium, 4% iron
Exchanges: 1½ Starch, ½ High-Fat Meat, ½ Fat

38

To Snack or Not to Snack

Snacking plays a key role in a healthy diet, especially if you have a finicky eater or a growing young athlete at your table. Experts tend to agree that snacking on good-for-you foods helps your growing children get adequate nutrients without adding extra calories. In fact, if chosen wisely, snacking may prevent your child from overeating at the next meal.

Crispy Cheese Chips

Layer wonton wrappers with garlic, basil, and Parmesan cheese for chips that provide big flavor and limited fat. Look for wonton wrappers in the refrigerated area of the produce section.

Prep: 30 minutes   Bake: 8 minutes per batch
Oven: 350°F   Makes: 60 chips (15 servings)

30 **wonton wrappers**
   Nonstick cooking spray
2 **tablespoons olive oil**
1 **clove garlic, minced**
½ **teaspoon dried basil, crushed**
¼ **cup grated Parmesan or Romano cheese**

1. Use a sharp knife to cut wonton wrappers diagonally in half to make 60 triangles. Lightly coat a baking sheet with cooking spray. Arrange one-third of the triangles in a single layer on the prepared baking sheet. If desired, for ruffled chips, line baking sheet with foil. Shape foil to make ridges. Lightly coat foil with cooking spray. Place wonton triangles on foil, draping over foil ridges.

2. In a small bowl stir together the olive oil, garlic, and basil. Lightly brush the wonton triangles with one-third of the oil mixture; sprinkle with one-third of the cheese.

3. Bake in a 350° oven about 8 minutes or until golden. Cool completely on a wire rack. Repeat with the remaining wonton triangles, oil mixture, and cheese.

Nutrition Facts per serving (4 chips): 69 cal., 2 g total fat (1 g sat. fat), 2 mg chol., 116 mg sodium, 9 g carbo., 0 g fiber, 2 g pro.
Daily Values: 3% calcium, 3% iron
Exchanges: ½ Starch, ½ Fat

Double Dippin' Fruit

Dip makes everything taste better to children. Get them eating fresh fruit by letting them dip it twice—once in creamy caramel sauce and then in crunchy low-fat granola.

Start to Finish: 15 minutes   *Makes:* 6 servings

1 **4-ounce container vanilla pudding (prepared pudding cup)**
3 **tablespoons caramel ice cream topping**
½ **teaspoon vanilla**
¼ **of an 8-ounce container frozen light whipped dessert topping, thawed**
¾ **cup low-fat granola**
Assorted fresh fruit such as sliced apples, banana chunks, or strawberries

1. For caramel dip, in a medium bowl combine pudding, caramel topping, and vanilla; stir until smooth. Fold in whipped topping.

2. To serve, spoon caramel dip into a serving bowl. Place granola in another serving bowl. Serve with fruit. Dip fruit in caramel dip and then in granola.

40

Nutrition Facts per serving: 129 cal., 3 g total fat (2 g sat. fat), 0 mg chol., 86 mg sodium, 24 g carbo., 1 g fiber, 1 g pro.
Daily Values: 4% vit. A, 1% vit. C, 2% calcium, 3% iron
Exchanges: 1 Fruit, ½ Other Carbo., ½ Fat

Peanutty Chocolate Spread

Looking for a quick answer to the munchies? Smear a little of this chocolate and peanut butter spread between cookies or crackers. Or stir in a little more yogurt and use it as a fruit dip.

Start to Finish: 15 minutes   *Makes:* 16 servings

- ½ **cup chunky peanut butter**
- ¼ **cup plain low-fat yogurt**
- ¼ **cup chocolate-flavored syrup**
- ½ **teaspoon vanilla**
- 32 **vanilla wafers or 16 graham cracker squares**
- 1 **cup assorted fresh fruit such as pineapple chunks, sliced strawberries, sliced bananas, and/or sliced apples**

1. For spread, in a medium bowl stir together peanut butter, yogurt, chocolate syrup, and vanilla. Spread the chocolate spread on the flat side of a vanilla wafer; top with another wafer. Serve with fresh fruit. Store leftover spread in a tightly covered container in the refrigerator up to 3 days.

Nutrition Facts per serving: 100 cal., 6 g total fat (1 g sat. fat), 0 mg chol., 76 mg sodium, 10 g carbo., 1 g fiber, 3 g pro.
Daily Values: 9% vit. C, 1% calcium, 2% iron
Exchanges: ½ Other Carbo., ½ High-Fat Meat

Safari Dip

Stuff celery with this smooth-as-silk peanut butter and honey dip. Or if your children prefer dipping, serve with crunchy jicama sticks, carrots, apples, and pears.

Start to Finish: 10 minutes   Makes: twenty 1-tablespoon servings (1 1/4 cups)

- 1/2 **of an 8-ounce package reduced-fat cream cheese (Neufchâtel), softened**
- 1/2 **cup creamy peanut butter**
- 2 **to 3 tablespoons milk**
- 2 **teaspoons honey**
- **Celery sticks, animal crackers, and/or assorted dippers such as peeled jicama sticks, carrot sticks, apple wedges, pear wedges, or graham cracker sticks**

1. For dip, in a small mixing bowl beat cream cheese with an electric mixer on medium speed until smooth. Beat in peanut butter, milk, and honey until well combined and smooth. If desired, chill before serving.

2. To serve, spread dip in celery sticks and garnish with animal crackers and cut-up fresh fruit. Or serve with assorted dippers.

Nutrition Facts per 1 tablespoon dip with dippers: 65 cal., 5 g total fat (? g sat. fat), 4 mg chol., 59 mg sodium, 4 g carbo., 1 g fiber, 2 g pro.
Daily Values: 66% vit. A, 5% vit. C, 1% calcium, 1% iron
Exchanges: 1 Vegetable, 1 Fat

Tropical Fruit Cups

Fresh mango and strawberries layered with yogurt and whipped dessert topping make outrageous sundaes for youngsters and adults alike.

Start to Finish: 10 minutes   *Makes:* 2 servings

   1 **8-ounce container low-fat piña colada-flavored yogurt or other flavored low-fat yogurt**
   ¼ **teaspoon vanilla**
   ¼ **cup frozen light whipped dessert topping, thawed**
   1 **cup cubed mango or papaya**
   ½ **cup sliced fresh strawberries**
   1 **tablespoon coconut, toasted**
      Graham cracker sticks (optional)

1. In a small bowl stir together yogurt and vanilla. Fold in whipped topping.

2. Divide the mango between 2 parfait glasses. Top each with one-fourth of the yogurt mixture. Top with strawberries and remaining yogurt mixture. Sprinkle with coconut. If desired, garnish with graham cracker sticks. Serve immediately.

Nutrition Facts per serving: 219 cal., 4 g total fat (3 g sat. fat), 5 mg chol., 79 mg sodium, 42 g carbo., 3 g fiber, 6 g pro.
Daily Values: 65% vit. A, 73% vit. C, 19% calcium, 2% iron
Exchanges: ½ Milk, 2½ Fruit, ½ Fat

Turn Off the Tube!

It makes sense that too many hours in front of the TV may be contributing to the growing number of overweight couch potatoes, but recently researchers determined it may say a little about the quality of our diets as well.

The School of Nutrition, Science, and Policy at Tufts University found that children whose families routinely watched television during mealtimes ate more salty snacks and fewer fruits and vegetables than those who turned off the television when eating.

Yam and Jam Muffins

Sweet potatoes pack vitamin A into these sweet and spicy, yummy muffins. Your kids won't suspect this good-for-you-ingredient. Serve them as an after-school snack or even for dessert.

Prep: 20 minutes Bake: 18 minutes
Cool: 25 minutes Oven: 400°F Makes: 12 muffins

1¾ cups all-purpose flour
⅓ cup packed brown sugar
1½ teaspoons baking powder
½ teaspoon baking soda
1 teaspoon apple pie spice or
   ground cinnamon
¼ teaspoon salt
½ of a 17-ounce can sweet potatoes, drained
   (about 1 cup)
1 beaten egg
½ cup milk
⅓ cup fruit jam or preserves
   (such as plum, strawberry, peach, or apricot)
¼ cup cooking oil
1 recipe Jam Icing

1. Lightly grease twelve 2½-inch muffin cups or line with paper bake cups; set aside.

2. In a large bowl combine flour, brown sugar, baking powder, baking soda, apple pie spice, and salt. Make a well in center of flour mixture; set aside.

3. In another bowl mash the drained sweet potatoes with a fork. Stir in egg, milk, jam, and oil. Add sweet potato mixture all at once to flour mixture. Stir just until moistened (batter should be lumpy).

4. Spoon batter into prepared muffin cups, filling each about three-fourths full. Bake in a 400° oven for 18 to 20 minutes or until golden and a wooden toothpick inserted in centers comes out clean. Cool in muffin cups on a wire rack for 5 minutes. Remove from muffin cups. Cool slightly. Drizzle muffins with Jam Icing and, if desired, top with additional jam or preserves.

Jam Icing: In a small bowl stir together ¾ cup sifted powdered sugar, 1 tablespoon fruit jam or preserves (such as plum, strawberry, peach, or apricot), ¼ teaspoon vanilla, and enough milk (2 to 3 teaspoons) to make icing of drizzling consistency. Makes about ¼ cup.

Nutrition Facts per muffin: 215 cal., 6 g total fat (1 g sat. fat), 19 mg chol., 174 mg sodium, 39 g carbo., 1 g fiber, 3 g pro.
Daily Values: 24% vit. A, 5% vit. C, 6% calcium, 8% iron
Exchanges: 1 Starch, 1½ Other Carbo., 1 Fat

Fruit Sundae Cones

Instead of high-calorie ice cream cones, serve these refreshing, high-nutrient fruit cones to the little ones playing in your backyard. Coconut and a drizzle of strawberry puree make them naturally sweet. Choose your kids' favorite fruit to fill up the cones.

Start to Finish: 5 minutes *Makes:* 6 servings

¾ **cup cut-up strawberries**

3 **cups cut-up fruits, such as apples, bananas, cherries, seedless red grapes, kiwifruit, plums, and/or peaches**

6 **large waffle cones**

¼ **cup coconut, toasted (optional)**

1. Place strawberries in a blender container; cover and blend until smooth. Place desired fruit in bowl; gently toss together. Spoon fruit into cones. Drizzle with the strawberry puree. If desired, top with coconut.

Nutrition Facts per serving: 105 cal., 1 g total fat (0 g sat. fat), 0 mg chol., 25 mg sodium, 24 g carbo., 2 g fiber, 1 g pro.
Daily Values: 2% vit. A, 25% vit. C, 1% calcium, 5% iron
Exchanges: 1 Fruit, ½ Starch

46

Super Snack Ideas

Because hungry kids often eat what they find first, make nutritious munchies readily available by designating a shelf in your refrigerator and pantry, then keep it well-stocked. Here are a few ideas:

* Instead of cookies, buy graham crackers.
* Replace the regular chips with baked potato chips.
* Fill resealable bags with cut-up cucumbers, carrots, and cheese.
* Buy frozen fruit without sugar, or nonfat or lowfat frozen yogurt, or fruit juice bars.
* Keep frozen fruit, such as strawberries or peaches, on hand and mix with fat-free milk in a blender to make a smoothie.
* Carry healthful snacks with you in a backpack on planned trips. Dry cereal, trail mix, raisins, dried fruit, rice cakes, and baby carrots make great on-the-go snacks.

Sparkling Stars

Fruit juice adds extra vitamin C to these jiggly, wiggly star-shaped snacks. Children love to pick them up with their fingers and watch 'em wiggle before devouring them.

Prep: 20 minutes   Chill: 1 hour   Makes: 24 (2-inch) stars or 48 squares

> **3 3-ounce packages red, orange, yellow, or blue fruit-flavored gelatin**
>
> **3 envelopes unflavored gelatin**
>
> **4 cups apple juice, white grape juice, or water**

1. In a large bowl stir together flavored and unflavored gelatin; set aside.

2. In a medium saucepan bring the juice to boiling; pour into gelatin mixture in bowl. Stir constantly for several minutes or until completely dissolved. Pour mixture into a 13×9×2-inch baking pan. Chill about 1 hour or until gelatin is set. Use a cookie cutter to cut into star shapes or cut into 1½-inch squares.

Nutrition Facts per star: 63 cal., 0 g total fat (0 g sat. fat), 0 mg chol., 30 mg sodium, 14 g carbo., 0 g fiber, 2 g pro.
Daily Values: 29% vit. C, 1% iron
Exchanges: 1 Other Carbo.

Creamy Stars: Prepare gelatin as above, except use sparkling white grape-flavored gelatin and 3 cups water. When gelatin is dissolved, stir in 1 cup light dairy sour cream. Chill and serve the gelatin as directed.

Mango Magic Pops

Summertime means refreshing frozen treats for little ones. Serve healthful pops made from real fruit, fruit nectar, and low-fat yogurt. They'll be a popular request all season long.

Prep: 15 minutes   Freeze: 4 hours   Makes: 8 pops

    1 teaspoon unflavored gelatin
    ⅓ cup peach or apricot nectar
    2 6- or 8-ounce cartons vanilla or peach fat-free yogurt
    ⅓ of a 26-ounce jar refrigerated mango slices, drained, or one 8-ounce
      can peach slices, drained

1. In a small saucepan combine the unflavored gelatin and peach nectar. Let stand for 5 minutes. Cook and stir over medium heat until gelatin is dissolved.

2. In a blender container or food processor bowl combine gelatin mixture, yogurt, and drained mango slices. Cover and blend or process until smooth. Spoon mixture into eight 3-ounce paper cups. Cover each cup with foil. Cut a small slit in the center of each foil cover and insert a rounded wooden stick into each. Freeze pops for 4 to 6 hours or until firm.

3. To serve, remove the foil and tear paper cups away from pops.

Nutrition Facts per pop: 65 cal., 0 g total fat (0 g sat. fat), 0 mg chol., 26 mg sodium, 15 g carbo., 0 g fiber, 2 g pro.
Daily Values: 3% vit. A, 20% vit. C, 9% calcium, 2% iron
Exchanges: 1 Fruit

Turkey and Tomato Wraps

A turkey sandwich, without the bread, supplies muscle-building protein to your children's diet and keeps hunger at bay.

Start to Finish: 15 minutes   Makes: 4 servings (2 wraps per serving)

  4 butterhead lettuce leaves (Bibb or Boston)
  4 ounces very thinly sliced cooked turkey breast
  **2 teaspoons honey mustard or low-fat mayonnaise dressing
     or salad dressing**
  1 small roma tomato, halved and very thinly sliced

1. Place lettuce leaves on a flat surface. Cut leaves in half lengthwise and remove center vein.

2. Place ½ ounce turkey onto each leaf just below the center. Spread honey mustard over turkey. Top with tomato slices. Roll up, starting from a short side. Secure with wooden toothpicks.

Nutrition Facts per serving: 35 cal., 1 g total fat (0 g sat. fat), 11 mg chol., 338 mg sodium, 3 g carbo., 0 g fiber, 5 g pro.
Daily Values: 6% vit. A, 8% vit. C, 1% calcium, 2% iron
Exchanges: ½ Vegetable, 1 Very Lean Meat

Veggie-Filled Quesadillas

A perfect snack for health-conscious teenagers—these quesadillas showcase fresh sweet peppers, red onions, and reduced-fat cream cheese. Serve them for study time.

Prep: 20 minutes   Bake: 5 minutes
Oven: 425°F   Makes: 10 servings

- 2 **small green and/or red sweet peppers, cut into thin strips**
- 1 **small red onion, cut into thin 1-inch-long strips**
- 2 **teaspoons olive oil or cooking oil**
- ½ **teaspoon ground cumin**
- ½ **teaspoon chili powder**
- 2 **tablespoons snipped fresh parsley or cilantro**
- ⅓ **cup reduced-fat cream cheese (tub style)**
- 5 **6- to 7-inch flour tortillas**
- **Salsa (optional)**

1. In a large nonstick skillet cook sweet peppers and onion in 1 teaspoon of the oil for 3 to 5 minutes or until crisp-tender. Stir in cumin and chili powder. Cook and stir for 1 minute more. Stir in parsley. Set aside.

2. Spread cream cheese over half of 1 side of each tortilla. Top with pepper mixture. Fold tortilla in half over peppers, pressing gently.

3. Place tortillas on an ungreased large baking sheet. Brush tortillas with the remaining 1 teaspoon oil. Bake in a 425° oven for 5 minutes. Cut each quesadilla into 4 wedges. Serve warm. If desired, pass the salsa.

Nutrition Facts per serving: 85 cal., 3 g total fat (1 g sat. fat), 4 mg chol., 118 mg sodium, 11 g carbo., 1 g fiber, 2 g pro.
Daily Values: 6% vit. A, 21% vit. C, 4% calcium, 4% iron
Exchanges: ½ Vegetable, ½ Starch, ½ Fat

BROWN BAG LUNCHES

Rest assured your child will eat a healthy lunch with these sandwiches and salads. Crunchy PB and A Wrap puts a new spin on the peanut butter sandwich, while Star Bright Sandwiches are a surefire lunchtime hit.

3

Pineapple Coleslaw

Crunchy PB and A Wrap

Turn a modest peanut butter sandwich into the envy of the lunchroom—add a little sweet apple and crunchy granola, then roll it up into a swirl.

Start to Finish: 5 minutes   Makes: 4 servings

> **4 7- to 8-inch flour tortillas**
> 1/3 **cup peanut butter**
> 1 **cup chopped apple**
> 1/4 **cup low-fat granola**

1. Spread peanut butter over each tortilla. Sprinkle with apple and granola. Tightly roll up tortillas. Cut in half. Wrap tightly in plastic wrap. Pack in insulated containers.

Nutrition Facts per serving: 254 cal., 14 g total fat (3 g sat. fat), 0 mg chol., 234 mg sodium, 28 g carbo., 3 g fiber, 8 g pro.
Daily Values: 2% vit. A, 3% vit. C, 4% calcium, 9% iron
Exchanges: 1/2 Fruit, 1 1/2 Starch, 1/2 High-Fat Meat, 1 1/2 Fat

Champion Chicken Pockets

Low-fat yogurt and ranch salad dressing top cold chicken salad hiding in a pita half. This sandwich is a surefire brown bag winner.

Start to Finish: 15 minutes   Makes: 4 sandwiches

   ¼ **cup plain low-fat yogurt**
   ¼ **cup bottled reduced-fat ranch salad dressing**
   1½ **cups chopped cooked chicken or turkey**
   ½ **cup chopped broccoli**
   ¼ **cup shredded carrot**
   ¼ **cup chopped pecans or walnuts (optional)**
   2 **6- to 7-inch whole wheat pita bread rounds, halved crosswise**

1. In a small bowl stir together yogurt and ranch salad dressing.

2. In a medium bowl combine chicken, broccoli, carrot, and, if desired, nuts. Pour yogurt mixture over chicken; toss to coat. Spoon chicken mixture into pita halves. Wrap tightly in plastic wrap and chill up to 24 hours. Pack sandwiches in insulated containers with ice packs.

55

Nutrition Facts per serving: 231 cal., 8 g total fat (1 g sat. fat), 53 mg chol., 392 mg sodium, 21 g carbo., 3 g fiber, 20 g pro.
Daily Values: 47% vit. A, 18% vit. C, 5% calcium, 10% iron
Exchanges: ½ Vegetable, 1 Starch, 2 Lean Meat, ½ Fat

Dizzy Spiral Sandwich

Go round and round with cheese, shredded carrot, dried fruit, and your child's favorite deli meat spiral-wrapped in a flour tortilla. It's guaranteed to put an end to lunchtime blahs!

Start to Finish: 15 minutes   *Makes:* 1 serving

    1 slice reduced-fat American cheese, quartered
    1 ounce very thinly sliced cooked chicken, turkey, or lean beef
    1 7- to 8-inch flour tortilla
    2 teaspoons honey mustard
    ¼ cup shredded carrot
    2 teaspoons dried tart cherries or raisins

1. Layer cheese and chicken on tortilla. Spread the mustard on chicken. Top with carrot and cherries. Tightly roll up tortilla. Cut in half. Wrap tightly in plastic wrap. Pack in an insulated container with an ice pack.

Nutrition Facts per serving: 227 cal., 7 g total fat (3 g sat. fat), 35 mg chol., 495 mg sodium, 25 g carbo., 2 g fiber, 15 g pro.
Daily Values: 177% vit. A, 5% vit. C, 24% calcium, 8% iron
Exchanges: ½ Vegetable, 1½ Starch, 1½ Lean Meat

Brown Baggin' It

Children don't want to be considered unusual by their peers, and sometimes what's in the lunch bag is up for scrutiny by the lunch crowd. Take time the night before to work together with your child to pack a nutritious lunch that you feel good about and that isn't likely to be traded.

Scoop-It-Up Chicken Salad

This lunch won't get traded. Mini taco shells scoop up chicken salad spiked with salsa and cheddar cheese.

Prep: 10 minutes   Makes: 1 serving

- ⅓ **cup chopped or shredded cooked chicken or turkey**
- 2 **tablespoons chopped celery**
- 1 **tablespoon light mayonnaise dressing or salad dressing**
- 1 **tablespoon salsa**
- 1 **tablespoon shredded cheddar cheese**
- 4 **mini taco shells**

1. For chicken salad, in a small bowl combine chicken, celery, mayonnaise dressing, salsa, and cheese; toss to mix. Spoon into a container; cover tightly.

2. Wrap taco shells in plastic wrap. Pack chicken salad and taco shells in an insulated bag with an ice pack. To serve, use taco shells to scoop up salad.

Nutrition Facts per serving: 235 cal., 11 g total fat (3 g sat. fat), 53 mg chol., 348 mg sodium, 16 g carbo., 2 g fiber, 17 g pro.
Daily Values: 4% vit. A, 4% vit. C, 9% calcium, 6% iron
Exchanges: 1 Starch, 2 Lean Meat, 1 Fat

Inside-Out Turkey Tempters

Do the hokey pokey and turn these sandwiches inside out for a kid-pleasing lunch. All the sandwich fixin's are there, but the bread is on the inside and the meat is on the outside.

Start to Finish: 15 minutes   Makes: 4 servings

12 **thin slices cooked turkey breast or turkey ham**

½ **cup flavored reduced-fat cream cheese (½ of an 8-ounce tub)**

4 **small green onions, trimmed, and/or 1 medium carrot, cut into thin lengthwise strips**

4 **dill or bread-and-butter thin, lengthwise pickle slices**

4 **soft breadsticks (6 to 8 inches long)**

Leaf lettuce (optional)

1. Overlap three turkey slices so meat is the same length as the breadsticks. Spread meat with 2 tablespoons cream cheese. Place one green onion, one pickle slice, and one breadstick on edge of turkey. Roll up so meat is wrapped around breadstick. If desired, roll one or two lettuce leaves around outside of sandwich. Repeat with remaining ingredients to make 4 sandwiches.

2. Wrap each sandwich tightly in plastic wrap. Chill up to 24 hours. Pack in insulated containers with ice packs.

Nutrition Facts per serving: 228 cal., 6 g total fat (3 g sat. fat), 26 mg chol., 856 mg sodium, 28 g carbo., 1 g fiber, 14 g pro.
Daily Values: 9% vit. A, 5% vit. C, 13% calcium, 14% iron
Exchanges: 2 Starch, 1 Lean Meat

Swimming Tuna Sandwiches

Toss together four ready-to-go ingredients and spread in fish-shaped bread for a protein-packed sandwich that will keep "starving" kids going until after school. Use different cutters to keep the ho-hum out of lunchtime routines.

Start to Finish: 10 minutes   Makes: 2 servings

1 **3-ounce can chunk white tuna (water pack), drained and flaked**
½ **cup packaged shredded cabbage with carrot (coleslaw mix)**
2 **tablespoons plain low-fat yogurt**
2 **tablespoons bottled reduced-fat ranch salad dressing**
8 **thin slices whole grain bread**
  Capers, sliced pimiento-stuffed olives, and/or raisins (optional)

1. In a small bowl combine tuna and cabbage; toss to mix. Stir in yogurt and salad dressing.

2. Using a 4- to 4½-inch cookie cutter, cut fish or other shapes from bread slices. Save bread scraps for another use. Spread tuna mixture on half of the bread shapes. Top with remaining bread shapes. If desired, decorate sandwiches with capers, olives, and/or raisins. Wrap tightly in plastic wrap. Chill up to 24 hours. Pack in insulated containers with ice packs.

Nutrition Facts per serving: 228 cal., 7 g total fat (1 g sat. fat), 24 mg chol., 599 mg sodium, 27 g carbo., 3 g fiber, 16 g pro.
Daily Values: 1% vit. A, 10% vit. C, 9% calcium, 12% iron
Exchanges: ½ Vegetable, 1½ Starch, 1½ Very Lean Meat, 1 Fat

Traveling Tuna Subs

When kids are hungry and running on empty, this tuna-, cheese-, and vegetable-filled sandwich fuels them up. It supplies carbohydrates for quick energy, protein for muscle building, and vitamin A to enhance eyesight.

Prep: 20 minutes   Chill: 2 to 24 hours
Makes: 4 sandwiches

- ⅓ **cup low-fat mayonnaise dressing or salad dressing**
- 1½ **teaspoons prepared mustard**
- ¼ **teaspoon dried dill**
- **Dash ground black pepper**
- 1 **12-ounce can tuna (water pack), drained and flaked**
- ½ **cup chopped carrot, celery, or red sweet pepper**
- 4 **frankfurter buns, split**
- ½ **cup shredded reduced-fat cheddar cheese (2 ounces)**

1. In a medium bowl stir together mayonnaise dressing, mustard, dill, and pepper. Stir in tuna and carrot; set aside.

2. Use a fork to hollow out the tops and bottoms of the frankfurter buns, leaving ¼-inch shells. Sprinkle cheese into the hollowed-out bun bottoms. Spoon tuna mixture over cheese. Add bun tops. Wrap tightly in plastic wrap. Chill for 2 to 24 hours. Pack in insulated containers with ice packs.

Nutrition Facts per sandwich: 307 cal., 7 g total fat (3 g sat. fat), 39 mg chol., 858 mg sodium, 29 g carbo., 2 g fiber, 29 g pro.
Daily Values: 91% vit. A, 4% vit. C, 19% calcium, 17% iron
Exchanges: 2 Starch, 3 Very Lean Meat, 1 Fat

Chilly Pizza Roll

Do you have a kid who loves cold pizza for breakfast? Try this lower calorie version of pizza rolled into a cold sandwich for lunch. It's one entrée that will be requested again and again.

Prep: 25 minutes   Bake: 13 minutes   Cool: 1 hour
Chill: 4 to 24 hours   Oven: 400°F   Makes: 6 rolls

Nonstick cooking spray
Cornmeal (optional)
1 **10-ounce package refrigerated pizza dough**
1 **3.5-ounce package pizza-style Canadian-style bacon**
  (1½-inch diameter)
⅓ **cup pizza sauce**
3 **1-ounce pieces string cheese, cut in half crosswise**

1. Lightly coat a baking sheet with cooking spray. If desired, lightly sprinkle cornmeal over baking sheet. Set aside.

2. On a lightly floured surface, unroll pizza dough. Press dough to form a 13½×9-inch rectangle. Cut into six 4½×4½-inch squares. Place Canadian bacon in the center of each square. Top with pizza sauce and string cheese. Bring up two opposite edges and pinch to seal. Pinch ends to seal. Place, seam side down, on prepared baking sheet.

3. Bake in a 400° oven for 13 to 18 minutes or until golden brown. Remove to a wire rack; cool. Wrap each sandwich in plastic wrap; chill for 4 to 24 hours. Pack in insulated containers with ice packs.

Nutrition Facts per roll: 187 cal., 6 g total fat (2 g sat. fat), 16 mg chol., 613 mg sodium, 23 g carbo., 1 g fiber, 11 g pro.
Daily Values: 5% vit. A, 2% vit. C, 11% calcium, 8% iron
Exchanges: 1½ Starch, 1 Medium-Fat Meat

Star Bright Sandwiches

Bake several of the rolls in advance and store them in your freezer. You can serve up the meat and cheese sandwiches in a twinkling.

Prep: 35 minutes   Rise: 30 minutes   Bake: 10 minutes
Cool: 1 hour   Oven: 350°F   Makes: 4 sandwiches

Nonstick cooking spray

4 frozen white or wheat Texas-style rolls, thawed according to package directions

8 ounces thinly sliced cooked ham or turkey

4 slices reduced-fat American cheese (3 to 4 ounces)

2 tablespoons bottled reduced-fat ranch or creamy Italian salad dressing

1. Lightly coat a baking sheet with cooking spray; set aside. Flatten thawed rolls into 4-inch rounds. Using a 3½- to 4-inch cookie cutter, cut rolls into star shapes. If desired, shape small scraps of dough into balls. Moisten star points with water and attach dough balls to the points of the stars.

2. Place stars 2 inches apart on prepared baking sheet. Cover and let rise in a warm place until nearly double (30 to 40 minutes). Bake in a 350° oven for 10 to 12 minutes or until golden. Transfer rolls to a wire rack. Cool completely.

3. Split rolls in half. Layer ham and cheese on bottom halves of rolls. Using a sharp knife, trim meat and cheese even with edges of rolls. Spread with dressing and add top halves of rolls. Wrap each sandwich tightly in plastic wrap. Pack in insulated containers with ice packs.

Nutrition Facts per sandwich: 313 cal., 13 g total fat (3 g sat. fat), 45 mg chol., 1,307 mg sodium, 30 g carbo., 1 g fiber, 19 g pro.
Daily Values: 6% vit. A, 20% calcium, 13% iron
Exchanges: 2 Starch, 2 Lean Meat, 1 Fat

Crunchy Potato Salad

Kids like the crunch, while parents like the hearty doses of vitamins A and C provided by this salad. Vitamin A protects against infection and vitamin C enhances immune systems.

Prep: 15 minutes   Cook: 20 minutes   Chill: 2 to 48 hours   Makes: 4 (1/2-cup) servings

- 1 **medium potato**
- 1/4 **cup light mayonnaise dressing or salad dressing**
- 1/2 **teaspoon prepared mustard**
- 3/4 **cup shredded carrots**
- 1/4 **cup finely chopped red sweet pepper**
- 2 **tablespoons sliced green onion (1)**
- 1 **tablespoon sweet pickle relish**
- **Sweet pickle slices (optional)**

1. In a small saucepan cook potato, covered, in boiling water for 20 to 25 minutes or just until tender. Drain well; cool slightly. Peel and cube potato.

2. Meanwhile, for dressing, in a medium bowl stir together mayonnaise dressing and mustard. Add potato, carrots, sweet pepper, onion, and relish to dressing. Toss lightly to coat. Cover and chill for 2 to 48 hours.

3. Spoon into 4 containers; cover tightly. Pack in insulated containers with ice packs. If desired, serve with pickle slices.

Nutrition Facts per serving: 97 cal., 5 g total fat (1 g sat. fat), 5 mg chol., 129 mg sodium, 13 g carbo., 2 g fiber, 1 g pro.
Daily Values: 139% vit. A, 43% vit. C, 1% calcium, 3% iron
Exchanges: 1/2 Vegetable, 1/2 Starch, 1 Fat

Pineapple Coleslaw

Peanuts, which are high in good fats, make a flavorful and crunchy topping for this pineapple-speckled coleslaw.

Start to Finish: 10 minutes   *Makes:* 4 servings

1½ **cups packaged shredded cabbage with carrots (coleslaw mix)**
¼ **cup well-drained pineapple tidbits (juice pack)**
2 **tablespoons vanilla low-fat yogurt**
2 **tablespoons light mayonnaise dressing or salad dressing**
¼ **cup honey-roasted peanuts, chopped**

1. In a small bowl combine cabbage, pineapple, yogurt, and mayonnaise dressing; toss to mix. Spoon into 4 containers. Sprinkle with peanuts; cover tightly. Pack in insulated containers with ice packs.

Nutrition Facts per serving: 75 cal., 4 g total fat (1 g sat. fat), 2 mg chol., 109 mg sodium, 9 g carbo., 1 g fiber, 2 g pro.
Daily Values: 2% vit. A, 17% vit. C, 4% calcium, 2% iron
Exchanges: 1½ Vegetable, 1 Fat

66

Applesauce with Crispy Scoops

Eating applesauce is fun when you can scoop it up with cinnamon-sprinkled, crispy tortilla chips. This easy-to-tote, low-calorie dessert is a simple way to coax one more serving of fruit into your child's daily diet.

Prep: 20 minutes   Bake: 7 minutes   Cool: 1 hour   Oven: 375°F   Makes: 4 servings

- 2 **7- to 8-inch flour tortillas**
  Nonstick cooking spray
- 2 **teaspoons sugar**
- ¼ **teaspoon ground cinnamon**
- 4 **4-ounce cups fruit-flavored or plain applesauce**

1. Cut each tortilla into 8 wedges. Place on an ungreased baking sheet. Generously coat tortilla wedges with cooking spray. In a small bowl stir together sugar and cinnamon. Sprinkle over tortilla wedges. Bake in a 375° oven for 7 to 9 minutes or until light brown. Cool completely on a wire rack.

2. For each serving, place 4 tortilla wedges in a plastic bag. Pack 1 bag and a container of applesauce in an insulated container with an ice pack. Use tortilla wedges to scoop up applesauce.

Nutrition Facts per serving: 136 cal., 1 g total fat (0 g sat. fat), 0 mg chol., 60 mg sodium, 30 g carbo., 1 g fiber, 1 g pro.
Daily Values: 84% vit. C, 2% calcium, 5% iron
Exchanges: 1 Fruit, 1 Starch

TOSS-TOGETHER SALADS

Colorful and crunchy, these refreshing salads entice children to eat vitamin-rich fruits and veggies. Plan a meal around a main-dish salad such as Turkey Taco Salad or choose Berry-Best Salad for a fruity side.

4

Turkey Taco Salad

BLT in a Bowl

This salad's star ingredients—savory bacon, crisp lettuce, and succulent tomatoes—are inspired by an all-time-favorite sandwich.

Start to Finish: 30 minutes   Oven: 450°F
Makes: 4 main-dish servings

8 thin slices **French bread (baguette-style)**

1 **tablespoon butter or margarine, melted**

2 **teaspoons snipped fresh parsley**

⅛ **teaspoon garlic salt**

6 **cups torn greens, such as iceberg, romaine, and/or spinach**

1½ **cups grape tomatoes or 3 roma tomatoes, seeded and chopped (1 cup)**

1 **small cucumber, halved lengthwise and thinly sliced**

½ **cup cubed mozzarella or Muenster cheese (2 ounces)**

8 **slices turkey bacon or bacon, crisp-cooked, drained, and crumbled**

¼ **cup bottled reduced-fat ranch, Italian, or French salad dressing**

1. For garlic toasts, place bread slices on a baking sheet. Bake in a 450° oven about 5 minutes or until toasted. Meanwhile, stir together butter, parsley, and garlic salt. Turn bread slices over; brush with butter mixture. Bake about 3 minutes more or until toasted; set aside.

2. Divide torn greens among 4 salad bowls or plates. Arrange tomatoes, cucumber, cheese, and bacon on the greens. Serve with dressing and garlic toasts.

Nutrition Facts per serving: 282 cal., 15 g total fat (5 g sat. fat), 41 mg chol., 909 mg sodium, 26 g carbo., 3 g fiber, 12 g pro.
Daily Values: 20% vit. A, 31% vit. C, 14% calcium, 10% iron
Exchanges: 2 Vegetable, 1 Starch, 1 Medium-Fat Meat, 2 Fat

Wheelie Ham Salad

Pop a wheelie at the dinner table! Serve this pasta salad loaded with summer zucchini, savory ham, and juicy tomatoes.

Prep: 25 minutes   Chill: 2 to 24 hours   Makes: 4 main-dish servings

> 4 ounces dried wagon wheel pasta (1½ cups)
> 4 ounces cooked lean ham, cut into bite-size pieces
> 1 small zucchini, quartered lengthwise and sliced
> 2 tablespoons sliced green onion (optional)
> ⅓ cup bottled reduced-fat ranch salad dressing
> 2 tablespoons plain low-fat yogurt
> 1 teaspoon dried basil, crushed
> ¾ cup grape or cherry tomatoes, halved

1. In a large saucepan cook pasta according to package directions. Drain. Rinse with cold water. Drain again. In a large bowl combine cooked pasta, ham, zucchini, and, if desired, green onion.

2. For dressing, in a small bowl stir together salad dressing, yogurt, and basil. Pour dressing over pasta mixture. Toss lightly to coat. Cover and chill for 2 to 24 hours. Before serving, gently stir tomatoes into pasta mixture.

Nutrition Facts per serving: 214 cal., 8 g total fat (1 g sat. fat), 23 mg chol., 596 mg sodium, 27 g carbo., 2 g fiber, 10 g pro.
Daily Values: 7% vit. A, 16% vit. C, 3% calcium, 10% iron
Exchanges: 1 Vegetable, 1½ Starch, ½ Lean Meat, 1 Fat

Tuna-Topped Tomatoes

Light mayonnaise dresses this version of an adored family salad.
Serve it for Saturday lunch before the big soccer game.

Prep: 15 minutes   Chill: 1 hour   Makes: 4 main-dish servings

- 1 cup chopped celery and/or chopped, seeded cucumber
- ½ cup shredded carrot (1 medium)
- 2 tablespoons sliced green onion (1)
- ⅓ cup light mayonnaise dressing or salad dressing
- 1½ teaspoons snipped fresh dill or ½ teaspoon dried dill
- ½ teaspoon finely shredded lemon peel
- ⅛ teaspoon garlic powder
- ⅛ teaspoon black pepper
- 1 6½-ounce can chunk light or white tuna (water pack), drained and broken into chunks
- 4 medium tomatoes, sliced

1. In a medium bowl combine celery, carrot, and green onion. Stir in mayonnaise dressing, dill, lemon peel, garlic powder, and pepper. Gently stir in tuna. Cover and chill for 1 to 4 hours. To serve, arrange sliced tomatoes on 4 plates. Spoon tuna mixture over tomato slices.

Nutrition Facts per serving: 124 cal., 2 g total fat (0 g sat. fat), 18 mg chol., 382 mg sodium, 14 g carbo., 3 g fiber, 13 g pro.
Daily Values: 96% vit. A, 48% vit. C, 4% calcium, 10% iron
Exchanges: 2½ Vegetable, 1½ Very Lean Meat, ½ Fat

Dieting Dilemma

With all of the emphasis on slim bodies, girls are dieting much earlier than their mothers ever thought about whittling away their waistlines. The result? According to a University of Texas study, ninth grade girls from California who were dieting or using weight-loss techniques such as laxatives, vomiting, or appetite suppressants were actually more likely to gain weight over four years than those classmates who weren't trying to lose.

Turkey Taco Salad

Ground turkey and baked tortilla chips keep this south-of-the-border salad lean, while pinto beans and corn add beneficial fiber.

Start to Finish: 25 minutes   Makes: 4 main-dish servings

Nonstick cooking spray

12 **ounces uncooked ground turkey**

1 **15-ounce can pinto beans, rinsed and drained (optional)**

1 **cup frozen whole kernel corn**

1 **cup bottled salsa**

¼ **cup water**

4 to 6 **cups shredded lettuce**

¼ **cup shredded reduced-fat cheddar cheese (1 ounce)**

1 **cup broken purchased baked tortilla chips**

1. Lightly coat a large nonstick skillet with cooking spray. Heat over medium heat. Cook ground turkey in hot skillet about 5 minutes or until no longer pink. Drain off any fat. Stir in beans (if desired), corn, salsa, and water. Bring to boiling; reduce heat. Simmer, covered, for 2 to 3 minutes to blend flavors.

2. Line 4 salad bowls or plates with lettuce. Top with hot turkey mixture. Sprinkle with cheese and tortilla chips. Serve immediately.

73

Nutrition Facts per serving: 275 cal., 9 g total fat (3 g sat. fat), 59 mg chol., 676 mg sodium, 29 g carbo., 3 g fiber, 23 g pro.
Daily Values: 13% vit. A, 21% vit. C, 13% calcium, 7% iron
Exchanges: 1½ Vegetable, 1½ Starch, 2 Lean Meat

Chilly Bow Ties and Tuna

Bow tie pasta, mandarin oranges, and Italian salad dressing take the ho-hum out of tuna salad. It's perfect for lunch on a warm summer day.

Prep: 20 minutes   Chill: 4 to 24 hours   Makes: 6 main-dish servings

   8 ounces dried farfalle pasta (bow ties)
  ⅓ cup light mayonnaise dressing or salad dressing
  ⅓ cup bottled reduced-calorie Italian salad dressing
  ¼ cup thinly sliced green onions (optional)
   2 tablespoons orange juice
  ¼ teaspoon salt
  ¼ teaspoon black pepper
   1 11-ounce can mandarin orange sections, drained
   1 12-ounce can chunk white tuna (water pack), drained and broken into chunks
   1 cup fresh pea pods, halved
    Milk (optional)

1. In a large saucepan cook pasta according to package directions. Drain. Rinse with cold water. Drain again.

2. Meanwhile, for dressing, in a large bowl combine mayonnaise dressing, Italian dressing, green onions (if desired), orange juice, salt, and pepper.

3. Add cooked pasta to dressing. Toss well to combine. Gently stir in orange sections, tuna, and pea pods. Cover and chill for 4 to 24 hours. Before serving, if necessary, stir in a little milk to moisten.

Nutrition Facts per serving: 254 cal., 3 g total fat (1 g sat. fat), 13 mg chol., 433 mg sodium, 43 g carbo., 2 g fiber, 13 g pro.
Daily Values: 11% vit. A, 24% vit. C, 3% calcium, 12% iron
Exchanges: ½ Fruit, 2½ Starch, 1 Very Lean Meat

Terrific Tortellini Salad

Brightly colored vegetables lurking among cheese-filled tortellini transform even picky eaters into vegetable eaters.

Prep: *20 minutes*   Chill: *2 to 24 hours*   Makes: *8 main-dish servings*

   1 **9-ounce package refrigerated light cheese tortellini or ravioli**
   3 **cups broccoli florets**
   1 **cup crinkle-cut or sliced carrots (2 medium)**
   ¼ **cup sliced green onions (2)**
   ½ **cup bottled reduced-fat ranch salad dressing**
   1 **large tomato, chopped**
   1 **cup fresh pea pods, halved**
   Milk (optional)

1. In a large saucepan cook pasta according to package directions. Add the broccoli and carrots during the last 3 minutes of cooking. Drain. Rinse with cold water. Drain again.

2. In a large bowl combine the cooked pasta mixture and green onions; drizzle with dressing. Gently toss to coat. Cover and chill for 2 to 24 hours.

3. Before serving, gently stir tomato and pea pods into pasta mixture. If necessary, stir in a little milk to moisten.

Nutrition Facts per serving: 145 cal., 5 g total fat (1 g sat. fat), 17 mg chol., 344 mg sodium, 22 g carbo., 3 g fiber, 6 g pro.
Daily Values: 99% vit. A, 62% vit. C, 6% calcium, 6% iron
Exchanges: 1½ Vegetable, 1 Starch, ½ Fat

Confetti Rice Salad

Cabbage, tomato, dried cherries, honey-roasted peanuts, and green onion color this chilly salad. It makes a great side dish for grilled hamburgers or chicken breasts.

Start to Finish: 20 minutes   Makes: 4 side-dish servings

   1 **cup cold cooked rice**
   1 **cup shredded red or green cabbage**
   ½ **cup chopped tomato (1 medium)**
   ¼ **cup dried tart cherries**
   2 **tablespoons chopped honey-roasted peanuts**
   1 **tablespoon sliced green onion (optional)**
   ¼ **cup bottled low-fat sweet and spicy French salad dressing**

1. In a medium bowl combine rice, cabbage, tomato, cherries, peanuts, and, if desired, green onion; toss to mix. Drizzle with salad dressing; gently stir to coat.

Nutrition Facts per serving: 131 cal., 3 g total fat (0 g sat. fat), 0 mg chol., 139 mg sodium, 25 g carbo., 1 g fiber, 2 g pro.
Daily Values: 3% vit. A, 24% vit. C, 2% calcium, 4% iron
Exchanges: ½ Vegetable, ½ Fruit, 1 Starch, ½ Fat

Purple Coleslaw

Red cabbage mixed with shredded carrot and sparked with chopped pear gives a new color to coleslaw. If your family prefers traditional, make it with the green cabbage.

Start to Finish: 20 minutes   *Makes:* 6 side-dish servings

    3 **tablespoons plain low-fat yogurt**
    3 **tablespoons light mayonnaise dressing or salad dressing**
    1 **teaspoon sugar**
    1 **medium pear, cored and chopped**
    2 **teaspoons lemon juice**
 1½ **cups shredded red or green cabbage**
  ⅓ **cup shredded carrot (1 small)**

1. For dressing, in a small bowl stir together yogurt, mayonnaise dressing, and sugar.

2. Toss pear with lemon juice. In a large bowl combine pear, cabbage, and carrot. Pour dressing over cabbage mixture. Toss lightly to coat. Serve immediately or cover and chill up to 2 hours.

Nutrition Facts per serving: 40 cal., 1 g total fat (0 g sat. fat), 1 mg chol., 56 mg sodium, 9 g carbo., 1 g fiber, 1 g pro.
Daily Values: 35% vit. A, 21% vit. C, 3% calcium, 1% iron
Exchanges: ½ Vegetable, ½ Fruit

Fast Food Facts
Before you super-size that fast-food order, consider how much portion sizes have grown over the past 25 years: In 1977 a hamburger weighed 5.7 ounces. In 1996 it grew to 7 ounces—an increase of nearly 100 calories. Soft drinks also jumped from 13 to 20 ounces—an almost 90-calorie increase.

Brain Power Salad

It's a no-brainer that broccoli is good for you. It's a super source of vitamin C needed for improved immunity.

Prep: 20 minutes   Chill: 1 hour   Makes: 4 side-dish servings

- ¼ **cup low-fat mayonnaise dressing or salad dressing**
- 2 **teaspoons sugar**
- 1 **teaspoon cider vinegar**
- 2 **cups broccoli florets**
- ½ **cup shredded carrot (1 medium)**
- ¼ **cup shredded reduced-fat cheddar cheese (1 ounce)**
- ¼ **cup sliced water chestnuts, drained**
- 2 **tablespoons chopped red onion (optional)**
- 2 **tablespoons crumbled crisp-cooked bacon**

1. For dressing, in a small bowl stir together mayonnaise dressing, sugar, and vinegar.

2. In a medium bowl combine broccoli, carrot, cheese, water chestnuts, and, if desired, onion. Pour dressing over broccoli mixture; toss to coat. Sprinkle with bacon. Cover and chill for 1 to 5 hours.

Nutrition Facts per serving: 90 cal., 3 g total fat (1 g sat. fat), 11 mg chol., 326 mg sodium, 11 g carbo., 2 g fiber, 5 g pro.
Daily Values: 93% vit. A, 72% vit. C, 9% calcium, 4% iron
Exchanges: 2½ Vegetable, ½ Fat

Berry-Best Salad

Fish-shape crackers or sunflower seeds top this salad and attract young diners. Make it with tangy fresh berries in the summer or use mandarin orange sections in the winter.

Start to Finish: 15 minutes   Makes: 4 side-dish servings

¼ **cup orange juice**

1 **tablespoon salad oil**

2 **teaspoons honey mustard or Dijon-style mustard**

1 **teaspoon sugar**

¼ **teaspoon salt**

4 **cups torn lettuce**

1½ **cups fresh blueberries, raspberries, quartered strawberries, and/or canned mandarin orange sections, drained**

2 **tablespoons bite-size cheddar fish-shape or pretzel crackers or 1 tablespoon shelled sunflower seeds**

1. For dressing, in a screw-top jar combine orange juice, oil, mustard, sugar, and salt. Cover and shake until combined. Place lettuce in medium bowl. Drizzle with dressing; toss to coat. Divide lettuce among 4 plates.

2. Arrange fruit on lettuce. Sprinkle with crackers. Serve immediately.

Nutrition Facts per serving: 86 cal., 4 g total fat (1 g sat. fat), 0 mg chol., 208 mg sodium, 13 g carbo., 3 g fiber, 1 g pro.
Daily Values: 5% vit. A, 32% vit. C, 2% calcium, 4% iron
Exchanges: 1 Vegetable, ½ Fruit, 1 Fat

Fruit Cups with Strawberry Dressing

So light, so cool, and so colorful, this fruit salad can't be beat during the hot summer months. It's perfect for appetites of all ages, making it perfect for family reunions.

Start to Finish: 25 minutes   *Makes: 6 side-dish servings*

- 2 **cups cut-up strawberries and/or whole raspberries**
- ¼ **cup frozen orange juice concentrate, thawed**
- 2 **teaspoons sugar**
- 2 **kiwifruit, peeled and thinly sliced**
- 1 **orange, peeled and sectioned**
- 2 **bananas, sliced**
- 1 **medium peach, plum, or nectarine; sliced**
- 1 **small apple or pear, cored and sliced**

1. For dressing, in a blender container or food processor bowl place half of the berries, the orange juice concentrate, and sugar. Cover and blend or process until smooth; set aside.

2. In a large bowl combine kiwifruit, orange sections, bananas, peach slices, apple slices, and remaining berries. Serve fruit in bowls with dressing.

Nutrition Facts per serving: 120 cal., 1 g total fat (0 g sat. fat), 0 mg chol., 4 mg sodium, 29 g carbo., 4 g fiber, 2 g pro.
Daily Values: 6% vit. A, 136% vit. C, 3% calcium, 4% iron
Exchanges: 2 Fruit

Orange and Pineapple Salad

Don't hesitate to serve this marshmallow- and fruit-laden salad. It's a lightened version of a traditional family favorite.

Prep: 10 minutes *Chill:* 2 to 24 hours *Makes:* 4 side-dish servings

    1 **8-ounce can pineapple chunks (juice pack), drained**
    ½ **cup miniature marshmallows**
    ½ **cup light dairy sour cream**
    1 **11-ounce can mandarin orange sections, drained**
    1 **tablespoon coconut, toasted**

1. In a medium bowl stir together pineapple chunks, miniature marshmallows, and light dairy sour cream. Gently fold in mandarin orange sections.

2. Cover and chill the salad for 2 to 24 hours. Before serving, sprinkle with the coconut.

Nutrition Facts per serving: 138 cal., 3 g total fat (2 g sat. fat), 10 mg chol., 33 mg sodium, 26 g carbo., 1 g fiber, 3 g pro.
Daily Values: 18% vit. A, 54% vit. C, 8% calcium, 2% iron
Exchanges: 2 Fruit, ½ Fat

Johnny Appleseed Salad

Low-fat yogurt and low-fat mayonnaise replace the usual whipped cream and mayonnaise dressing in this Waldorf salad, slashing the fat by almost 90 percent.

Start to Finish: 15 minutes   *Makes:* 4 side-dish servings

> 2 **cups chopped apples (2 medium)**
> 1½ **teaspoons lemon juice**
> ¼ **cup raisins, dried cranberries, or mixed dried fruit bits**
> ¼ **cup seedless green grapes, halved**
> 2 **tablespoons sliced celery**
> ⅓ **cup orange or vanilla low-fat yogurt**
> 2 **tablespoons light mayonnaise dressing or salad dressing**
> 1 **tablespoon chopped walnuts or pecans**

1. In a medium bowl toss apples with lemon juice. Add raisins, grapes, and celery. Toss to mix.

2. For dressing, in a small bowl stir together yogurt and mayonnaise dressing. Add dressing to apple mixture; toss gently to coat. Serve immediately or cover and chill up to 8 hours. Before serving, sprinkle with nuts.

84

Nutrition Facts per serving: 113 cal., 2 g total fat (0 g sat. fat), 3 mg chol., 86 mg sodium, 24 g carbo., 2 g fiber, 2 g pro.
Daily Values: 2% vit. A, 10% vit. C, 5% calcium, 3% iron
Exchanges: 1½ Fruit, ½ Fat

Nuts-About-Fruit Salad

Need help getting your kids to eat fruit salad? Give this one a try—a little peanut butter whisked into the dressing works wonders.

Prep: 15 minutes   Chill: 1 hour   Makes: 6 side-dish servings

- 1 **8-ounce can crushed pineapple (juice pack)**
- 1 **cup shredded carrot**
- 1 **cup chopped apple or pear**
- ¼ **cup shelled sunflower seeds**
- ¼ **cup raisins or dried tart cherries**
- ⅓ **cup plain low-fat yogurt**
- 2 **tablespoons creamy peanut butter**

1. Drain pineapple, reserving 1 tablespoon juice. In a medium bowl combine pineapple, carrot, apple, sunflower seeds, and raisins.

2. For dressing, in a small bowl stir together yogurt and peanut butter until smooth. Stir in reserved pineapple juice. Pour dressing over pineapple mixture; toss gently to mix. Cover and chill for 1 to 4 hours.

Nutrition Facts per serving: 135 cal., 6 g total fat (1 g sat. fat), 1 mg chol., 43 mg sodium, 19 g carbo., 3 g fiber, 4 g pro.
Daily Values: 115% vit. A, 11% vit. C, 5% calcium, 5% iron
Exchanges: 1 Fruit, ½ High-Fat Meat, 5 Fat

WHAT'S FOR DINNER?

From slimmed-down take-offs on restaurant favorites to wholesome home-style soups, these main dishes score big with kids as well as Mom and Dad.

5

Crispy Chicken Nuggets
with Honey-Mustard Dip

Chili-Mac Skillet

A favorite ingredient combination, this lineup of lean ground beef, pasta, tomato sauce, and reduced-fat cheddar cheese hits a home run for family weeknight dinners.

Prep: 15 minutes   Cook: 20 minutes   Makes: 4 servings

- 8 ounces lean ground beef
- ½ cup finely chopped onion (1 medium)
- 1 8-ounce can tomato sauce
- 1 15-ounce can tomato puree
- 1 cup dried elbow macaroni
- ½ cup finely chopped green sweet pepper
- ¼ cup water
- 1 tablespoon chili powder
- ½ teaspoon garlic salt
- ½ cup shredded reduced-fat cheddar cheese (2 ounces)

1. In a large skillet cook ground beef and onion over medium-high heat until meat is brown and onion is tender. Drain off fat.

2. Stir in tomato sauce, tomato puree, uncooked macaroni, sweet pepper, water, chili powder, and garlic salt. Bring to boiling; reduce heat. Simmer, covered, about 20 minutes or until macaroni is tender, stirring often.

3. Remove skillet from heat; sprinkle with cheese. Cover and let stand about 2 minutes or until the cheese is melted.

Nutrition Facts per serving: 334 cal., 10 g total fat (5 g sat. fat), 57 mg chol., 676 mg sodium, 37 g carbo., 4 g fiber, 25 g pro.
Daily Values: 33% vit. A, 70% vit. C, 12% calcium, 22% iron
Exchanges: ½ Vegetable, 2 Starch, ½ Other Carbo., 2 Lean Meat

Layers of Lasagna

Layers of zesty-seasoned ground beef and tomatoes, tender pasta, and creamy ricotta cheese create a family-pleasing casserole. This version is lower in fat and provides generous amounts of both vitamin A and calcium.

Prep: *30 minutes*   Bake: *25 minutes*
Stand: *10 minutes*   Oven: *375°F*
Makes: *8 servings*

12 **ounces lean ground beef**
½ **cup chopped onion (1 medium)**
½ **cup finely chopped carrot**
2 **cloves garlic, minced**
1 **15-ounce can Italian-style tomato sauce**
1 **6-ounce can tomato paste**
¼ **teaspoon black pepper**
1 **beaten egg**
1 **15-ounce carton light ricotta cheese**
Nonstick cooking spray
9 **lasagna noodles, cooked and drained**
1 **cup shredded part-skim mozzarella cheese (4 ounces)**
¼ **cup grated Parmesan or Romano cheese (1 ounce)**

1. For sauce, in a large saucepan cook ground beef, onion, carrot, and garlic until meat is brown. Drain off fat. Stir in the tomato sauce, tomato paste, ½ cup water, and pepper. Bring to boiling; reduce heat. Simmer, covered, for 10 minutes, stirring occasionally.

2. For cheese filling, in a small bowl stir together the egg and ricotta cheese. Lightly coat a 2-quart rectangular baking dish with cooking spray. Layer 3 noodles in the prepared baking dish. Spread with a third of the cheese filling. Top with a third of the sauce and a third of the mozzarella cheese. Repeat layers twice. Sprinkle with Parmesan cheese.

3. Bake, covered, in a 375° oven for 20 minutes. Uncover and bake for 5 minutes more or until heated through. Let stand for 10 minutes before serving.

Nutrition Facts per serving: 299 cal., 10 g total fat (5 g sat. fat), 73 mg chol., 514 mg sodium, 28 g carbo., 3 g fiber, 25 g pro.
Daily Values: 42% vit. A, 17% vit. C, 39% calcium, 13% iron
Exchanges: ½ Vegetable, 1½ Starch, 3 Lean Meat

Beefy Italian Skillet

Slowly simmer beef round steak in herb-packed tomato and mushroom sauce for an entrée so tender it can be cut with a fork.

Prep: 35 minutes   Cook: 1¼ hours   Makes: 4 servings

1 pound boneless beef round steak
  Nonstick cooking spray
2 cups sliced fresh mushrooms
1 cup chopped onion (1 large)
1 cup coarsely chopped green sweet pepper
½ cup chopped celery (1 stalk)
2 cloves garlic, minced
1 14½-ounce can tomatoes, undrained and cut up
½ teaspoon dried basil, crushed
¼ teaspoon dried oregano, crushed
¼ teaspoon crushed red pepper (optional)
8 ounces dried spaghetti
2 tablespoons grated Parmesan cheese (optional)

1. Trim fat from meat. Cut meat into 4 serving-size pieces. Lightly coat an unheated large skillet with cooking spray. Heat over medium heat. Add meat to skillet; cook each piece on both sides until brown. Remove meat from skillet.

2. Add mushrooms, onion, sweet pepper, celery, and garlic to the skillet. Cook until vegetables are nearly tender. Stir in undrained tomatoes, basil, oregano, and, if desired, crushed red pepper. Add meat to skillet, spooning vegetable mixture over the meat. Simmer, covered, about 1¼ hours or until meat is tender, stirring occasionally. Meanwhile, cook spaghetti according to package directions.

3. Transfer meat to a serving platter. Spoon vegetable mixture over meat. Serve with spaghetti. If desired, sprinkle with Parmesan cheese.

Nutrition Facts per serving: 438 cal., 8 g total fat (3 g sat. fat), 56 mg chol., 273 mg sodium, 55 g carbo., 4 g fiber, 37 g pro.
Daily Values: 17% vit. A, 67% vit. C, 10% calcium, 30% iron
Exchanges: 2½ Vegetable, 2½ Starch, 3 Lean Meat

My Own Pasta Bake

For almost instant protection against growling stomachs, freeze this beloved Italian casserole in portion-size containers. Zap it in the microwave and douse pangs of hunger in a few minutes.

Prep: 30 minutes Bake: 20 minutes Oven: 375°F Makes: 6 servings

8 ounces dried penne

1 14-ounce can whole Italian-style tomatoes, undrained

½ of a 6-ounce can (⅓ cup) Italian-style tomato paste

¼ cup tomato juice

½ teaspoon sugar

½ teaspoon dried oregano, crushed, or 2 teaspoons snipped fresh oregano

¼ teaspoon black pepper

1 pound lean ground beef

½ cup chopped onion (1 medium)

¼ cup sliced pitted ripe olives

½ cup shredded reduced-fat mozzarella cheese (2 ounces)

1. Cook pasta according to package directions. Drain; set aside.

2. Meanwhile, in a blender container or food processor bowl combine undrained tomatoes, tomato paste, tomato juice, sugar, dried oregano (if using), and pepper. Cover and blend or process until smooth. Set aside.

3. In a large skillet cook ground beef and onion over medium-high heat until meat is brown. Drain off fat. Stir in tomato mixture. Bring to boiling; reduce heat. Simmer, covered, for 10 minutes. Stir in pasta, fresh oregano (if using), and olives.

4. Divide the pasta mixture among six 10- to 12-ounce casseroles. Bake, covered, in a 375° oven for 15 minutes. (Or spoon all of the pasta mixture into a 2-quart casserole. Bake, covered, for 30 minutes.) Sprinkle with mozzarella cheese. Bake, uncovered, about 5 minutes more or until cheese is melted.

91

Nutrition Facts per serving: 330 cal., 10 g total fat (4 g sat. fat), 51 mg chol., 442 mg sodium, 36 g carbo., 2 g fiber, 22 g pro.
Daily Values: 22% vit. A, 21% vit. C, 10% calcium, 23% iron
Exchanges: 1 Vegetable, 2 Starch, 1 Lean Meat

Cheesy Polenta with Meat Sauce

Little ones heartily approve of the soft polenta hiding beneath the beef-and-marinara sauce. One serving supplies complex carbohydrates, protein, and a little fat to help stabilize blood sugar levels and moods.

Prep: 15 minutes   Bake: 30 minutes   Oven: 350°F   Makes: 6 servings

Nonstick cooking spray
8 ounces lean ground beef
1 15-ounce container refrigerated marinara sauce
1 16-ounce tube refrigerated cooked plain polenta
¾ cup shredded Italian 4-cheese blend (3 ounces)

1. Lightly coat a 2-quart square baking dish with cooking spray. In a large skillet cook ground beef over medium-high heat until brown; drain off fat. Stir in marinara sauce; set aside.

2. Cut polenta into ½-inch slices. Arrange polenta slices in the bottom of the prepared baking dish. Sprinkle with ½ cup of the cheese. Spoon meat sauce evenly over polenta.

3. Bake, covered, in a 350° oven about 30 minutes or until heated through. Sprinkle with the remaining ¼ cup cheese. Let stand for 1 to 2 minutes or until cheese is melted.

Nutrition Facts per serving: 184 cal., 10 g total fat (4 g sat. fat), 39 mg chol., 458 mg sodium, 10 g carbo., 0 g fiber, 13 g pro.
Daily Values: 2% vit. A, 12% calcium, 5% iron
Exchanges: ½ Starch, 2 Lean Meat, ½ Fat

Sloppy Salsa Joes

These are definitely not the sloppy joes you ate while growing up. Fresh vegetables in the spicy salsa-meat mixture add texture and extra nutrients—your kids won't even notice.

Start to Finish: 30 minutes   *Makes:* 6 to 8 servings

- 1 **pound lean ground beef**
- ½ **cup chopped onion (1 medium)**
- 2 **cloves garlic, minced**
- 1 **cup chopped zucchini**
- 1 **cup chopped yellow summer squash**
- 1 **cup sliced fresh mushrooms**
- ¾ **cup chopped green sweet pepper (1 medium)**
- 1 **16-ounce jar salsa**
- 1 **teaspoon dried basil, crushed**
- ½ **teaspoon dried parsley flakes**
- ½ **teaspoon dried rosemary, crushed**
- 6 to 8 **kaiser rolls, split and toasted**

1. In a large skillet cook ground beef, onion, and garlic over medium-high heat until meat is brown. Drain off fat. Stir in zucchini, yellow summer squash, mushrooms, and sweet pepper. Cook, covered, over low heat for 5 to 7 minutes or until vegetables are tender.

2. Stir in salsa, basil, parsley, and rosemary. Bring to boiling; reduce heat. Simmer, uncovered, about 10 minutes or until most of the liquid has evaporated. Serve on toasted rolls.

Nutrition Facts per serving: 379 cal., 10 g total fat (3 g sat. fat), 48 mg chol., 915 mg sodium, 50 g carbo., 4 g fiber, 22 g pro.
Daily Values: 14% vit. A, 51% vit. C, 10% calcium, 21% iron
Exchanges: 2 Vegetable, 2½ Starch, 2 Lean Meat

Festive Taco Burgers

Ordinary burgers make a Mexican festival when they're spiced with chile peppers, oregano, and cumin, then topped with tomato salsa and wrapped in flour tortillas.

Prep: 20 minutes *Bake:* 15 minutes *Broil:* 10 minutes *Oven:* 350°F *Makes:* 5 servings

- 1 cup finely chopped tomato (2 medium)
- ¼ cup green or red taco sauce
- 2 tablespoons snipped fresh cilantro
- 5 7-inch flour tortillas
- 1 4-ounce can diced mild green chile peppers, drained
- ¼ cup fine dry bread crumbs
- ¼ cup finely chopped green onions (2)
- 2 tablespoons milk
- 1 teaspoon dried oregano, crushed
- ½ teaspoon ground cumin
- ¼ teaspoon black pepper
- ⅛ teaspoon salt
- 1 pound lean ground beef
- Nonstick cooking spray
- 1 cup shredded lettuce or red cabbage

1. In a medium bowl stir together tomato, taco sauce, and cilantro. Cover and set aside. Wrap the tortillas in foil; heat in a 350° oven for 15 minutes. Remove from oven, but do not open foil packet.

2. Meanwhile, in a large bowl stir together the chile peppers, bread crumbs, green onions, milk, oregano, cumin, black pepper, and salt. Add ground beef; mix well. Shape mixture into 5 oval patties about 4½ to 5 inches long and ½ inch thick. Lightly coat the unheated rack of a broiler pan with cooking spray; arrange patties on broiler pan. Broil 3 to 4 inches from the heat for 10 to 12 minutes or until done (160°F), turning once halfway through broiling.

3. To serve, place a patty on each warm tortilla; spoon some of the shredded lettuce and tomato mixture over the patty. Wrap tortillas around patties.

Nutrition Facts per serving: 293 cal., 12 g total fat (4 g sat. fat), 58 mg chol., 408 mg sodium, 24 g carbo., 3 g fiber, 21 g pro.
Daily Values: 14% vit. A, 38% vit. C, 10% calcium, 22% iron
Exchanges: 1 Vegetable, 1 Starch, ½ Other Carbo., 3 Lean Meat

Family-Style Chili

Your kids will say "adios" to canned soups once they've tasted this mildly seasoned chili. It's full of beans high in soluble fiber that helps to regulate blood sugar levels.

Prep: 25 minutes   Cook: 25 minutes   Makes: 4 servings (about 5 cups)

8 ounces lean ground beef
1 cup chopped onion (1 large)
½ cup chopped celery (1 stalk)
½ cup chopped green sweet pepper
2 cloves garlic, minced
1 15-ounce can red kidney beans, rinsed and drained (optional)
1 15-ounce can tomato puree
1 11½-ounce can tomato juice
½ cup water
2 teaspoons chili powder
1 teaspoon sugar (optional)
½ teaspoon dried basil, crushed
¼ teaspoon salt
Shredded reduced-fat cheddar cheese (optional)

1. In a large saucepan cook ground beef, onion, celery, sweet pepper, and garlic over medium-high heat until meat is brown and onion is tender. Drain off fat.

2. Stir in the kidney beans (if using), tomato puree, tomato juice, water, chili powder, sugar (if desired), basil, and salt. Bring to boiling; reduce heat. Simmer, covered, for 25 to 30 minutes or until the vegetables are tender. Season to taste with salt and black pepper. If desired, top each serving with cheese.

Nutrition Facts per serving: 167 cal., 6 g total fat (2 g sat. fat), 36 mg chol., 509 mg sodium, 16 g carbo., 3 g fiber, 13 g pro.
Daily Values: 21% vit. A, 80% vit. C, 3% calcium, 14% iron
Exchanges: 1 Vegetable, ½ Starch, 2 Very Lean Meat, 1 Fat

Fast Fajita Roll-Ups

Just 20 minutes from start to finish makes these fajitas great for dinner before dance lessons, basketball practices, football games, band rehearsals, or whatever keeps your busy family on the run.

Start to Finish: 20 minutes   Oven: 350°F
Makes: 4 servings

12 ounces beef flank steak or sirloin steak or skinless, boneless chicken breast halves

4 8-inch spinach or flour tortillas

1 tablespoon cooking oil

⅓ cup finely chopped onion (1 small)

⅓ cup finely chopped green sweet pepper

½ cup chopped tomato (1 medium)

2 tablespoons bottled reduced-fat Italian salad dressing

½ cup shredded reduced-fat cheddar cheese (2 ounces)

¼ cup bottled salsa or taco sauce

¼ cup light dairy sour cream (optional)

1. If desired, partially freeze beef for easier slicing. Trim fat from steak. Cut beef or chicken into bite-size strips.

2. Wrap tortillas tightly in foil. Heat in a 350° oven about 10 minutes or until heated through. Meanwhile, heat oil in a 12-inch skillet over medium-high heat. Add meat, onion, and sweet pepper; cook and stir for 2 to 3 minutes or until desired doneness for steak or until chicken is no longer pink. Remove from heat. Drain well. Stir in tomato and salad dressing.

3. To serve, fill warm tortillas with meat mixture. Roll up tortillas. Serve with cheese, salsa, and, if desired, sour cream.

Nutrition Facts per serving: 324 cal., 15 g total fat (6 g sat. fat), 43 mg chol., 462 mg sodium, 21 g carbo., 2 g fiber, 24 g pro.
Daily Values: 9% vit. A, 31% vit. C, 15% calcium, 14% iron
Exchanges: 1 Vegetable, 1 Starch, 3 Lean Meat, 1 Fat

Pineapple Beef

Sweet and pungent Asian flavors glaze the tender beef strips and delectable pineapple in this family-friendly stir-fry.

Prep: 15 minutes   Cook: 5 minutes   Marinate: 15 minutes   Makes: 4 servings

   12 **ounces beef top round steak**
    1 **8-ounce can pineapple slices (juice pack)**
    2 **tablespoons reduced-sodium soy sauce**
   ½ **teaspoon grated fresh ginger or ⅛ teaspoon ground ginger**
   ¼ **teaspoon crushed red pepper**
    1 **tablespoon cornstarch**
      Nonstick cooking spray
    4 **green onions, cut into ½-inch pieces**
    1 **6-ounce package frozen pea pods**
    1 **medium tomato, cut into wedges**
    2 **cups hot cooked rice**

1. If desired, partially freeze meat for easier slicing. Trim fat from meat. Thinly slice meat across the grain into bite-size strips. Drain pineapple, reserving juice. Cut pineapple slices into quarters. Set aside.

2. In a bowl stir together reserved pineapple juice, soy sauce, ginger, and crushed red pepper. Add the meat; stir until coated. Cover and marinate meat at room temperature for 15 minutes. Drain, reserving marinade. For sauce, stir cornstarch into reserved marinade. Set aside.

3. Lightly coat an unheated large nonstick skillet or wok with cooking spray. Heat over medium heat. Add meat and green onions. Cook and stir for 2 to 3 minutes or until meat is desired doneness. Push from center of skillet.

4. Stir sauce; add to center of skillet. Cook and stir over medium heat until thickened and bubbly. Add pineapple, pea pods, and tomato. Cook and stir for 2 minutes more. Serve immediately over hot cooked rice.

Nutrition Facts per serving: 284 cal., 2 g total fat (1 g sat. fat), 37 mg chol., 340 mg sodium, 39 g carbo., 3 g fiber, 24 g pro.
Daily Values: 8% vit. A, 26% vit. C, 6% calcium, 20% iron
Exchanges: 1 Vegetable, ½ Fruit, 1½ Starch, 2½ Very Lean Meat

Pork Lo Mein

Trying to sneak some extra vegetables into your kids' diets? Serve them this Asian main dish. Carrots, sweet peppers, and mushrooms will creep into their mouths along with savory ground pork and fun-to-eat spaghetti.

Start to Finish: 35 minutes   Makes: 4 servings

> 12 ounces ground pork*
> 2 cups sliced fresh mushrooms
> 1 cup shredded or biased-sliced carrots (2 medium)
> ½ cup red and/or green sweet pepper cut into bite-size strips
> 2 cloves garlic, minced
> 1 tablespoon cornstarch
> 1 cup reduced-sodium chicken broth
> 1 tablespoon reduced-sodium soy sauce
> 1 teaspoon grated fresh ginger
> ¼ teaspoon crushed red pepper
> ¼ teaspoon curry powder
> 4 ounces dried thin spaghetti or linguine, broken, cooked, and drained
> 1 cup fresh bean sprouts
> ½ cup sliced green onions (4)
> Sliced green onion (optional)

1. In a large skillet cook pork, mushrooms, carrots, sweet pepper, and garlic over medium-high heat until meat is brown and vegetables are tender. Drain off fat.

2. Stir cornstarch into meat mixture. Stir in broth, soy sauce, ginger, crushed red pepper, and curry powder. Cook and stir until thickened and bubbly. Cook and stir for 2 minutes more.

3. Stir in cooked pasta, bean sprouts, and the ½ cup green onions; heat through. If desired, garnish with additional green onion.

*Note: If you prefer, substitute 12 ounces lean boneless pork, thinly sliced into bite-size strips, for the ground pork. To cook boneless pork, heat 1 teaspoon cooking oil in the large skillet over medium-high heat. Add the meat strips. Stir-fry for 2 to 3 minutes or until pork is no longer pink. Remove meat from skillet. Cook the mushrooms, carrot, sweet pepper, and garlic as directed. Return meat to skillet and continue as directed.

Nutrition Facts per serving: 345 cal., 15 g total fat (5 g sat. fat), 49 mg chol., 367 mg sodium, 31 g carbo., 3 g fiber, 21 g pro.
Daily Values: 161% vit. A, 63% vit. C, 5% calcium, 17% iron
Exchanges: 2 Vegetable, 1 Starch, 2 High-Fat Meat

Double-the-Meat Sandwiches

Leftovers take on new life when they're made into deli-style sandwiches with a masterfully blended mustard sauce—not too hot, not too sweet, and not too strong.

Start to Finish: 20 minutes   Makes: 6 servings

- ¼ **cup low-fat mayonnaise dressing or salad dressing**
- 1½ **teaspoons prepared mustard**
- 1½ **teaspoons honey**
- 1½ **teaspoons milk**
- ⅛ **teaspoon black pepper**
- 6 **dinner rolls (about 3 inches in diameter)**
- 8 **ounces thinly sliced cooked turkey or lean pork roast**
- 8 **ounces thinly sliced cooked ham**
- 1 **cup shredded lettuce**
- 6 **dill pickle slices or spears (optional)**

1. For mustard sauce, in a small bowl stir together mayonnaise dressing, mustard, honey, milk, and pepper; set aside.

2. On the bottom half of each roll, layer turkey, ham, and lettuce. Drizzle each with some of the mustard sauce. Add top halves of rolls. If desired, serve with pickles.

Nutrition Facts per serving: 211 cal., 7 g total fat (2 g sat. fat), 43 mg chol., 1,063 mg sodium, 21 g carbo., 1 g fiber, 16 g pro.
Daily Values: 6% vit. A, 5% vit. C, 5% calcium, 8% iron
Exchanges: 1½ Starch, 2 Lean Meat

Crispy Chicken Nuggets with Honey-Mustard Dip

Worried about how much fat is in your kids' favorite chicken nuggets? Make your own. These crispy nuggets are baked, not fried, keeping fat levels low.

Prep: 20 minutes   Bake: 10 minutes   Oven: 425°F   Makes: 4 servings

½ **cup low-fat mayonnaise dressing or salad dressing**
4 **teaspoons Dijon-style mustard**
1 **tablespoon honey**
1 **pound skinless, boneless chicken breast halves**
¼ **cup all-purpose flour**
1 **teaspoon dried parsley flakes**
½ **teaspoon poultry seasoning**
⅛ **teaspoon salt**
   Dash black pepper
1 **beaten egg**
2 **tablespoons milk**
30 **whole wheat or regular rich round crackers, finely crushed (1¼ cups)**

1. For honey-mustard dip, in a small bowl, stir together mayonnaise dressing, mustard, and honey. Cover and chill until serving time.

2. Cut chicken into 1½-inch pieces. In a plastic bag combine flour, parsley flakes, poultry seasoning, salt, and pepper. Add chicken pieces, a few at a time, to the flour mixture. Close the bag; shake to coat chicken pieces. Set chicken aside.

3. In a bowl stir together egg and milk. Place crushed crackers in another bowl. Dip coated chicken pieces, a few at a time, into the egg mixture. Roll the pieces in crackers. Place in a single layer on a large ungreased baking sheet. Bake in a 425° oven for 10 to 12 minutes or until chicken is no longer pink.

4. Serve with cold or warm honey-mustard dip. To warm dip, cover with waxed paper and microwave on 100 percent power (high) for 30 seconds or until heated through. (Or transfer dip to a small saucepan; heat and stir over low heat.)

Nutrition Facts per serving: 354 cal., 10 g total fat (2 g sat. fat), 126 mg chol., 637 mg sodium, 34 g carbo., 2 g fiber, 31 g pro.
Daily Values: 5% vit. A, 4% vit. C, 7% calcium, 16% iron
Exchanges: 2 Starch, 4 Very Lean Meat, 1½ Fat

Honey Crusted Chicken

Crispy baked chicken with a dynamite trio of flavors—honey, orange juice, and ginger—hits the spot with hungry kids.

Prep: 10 minutes   Bake: 18 minutes   Oven: 350°F   Makes: 4 servings

Nonstick cooking spray
4 small skinless, boneless chicken breast halves (about 1 pound)
1 tablespoon honey
1 tablespoon orange juice
¼ teaspoon ground ginger
¼ teaspoon black pepper
Dash cayenne pepper (optional)
¾ cup cornflakes, crushed (about ⅓ cup)
½ teaspoon dried parsley flakes (optional)

1. Lightly coat a shallow baking pan with cooking spray. Place chicken in baking pan.

2. In a small bowl combine the honey, orange juice, ginger, black pepper, and, if desired, cayenne pepper. Brush honey mixture over chicken.

3. Combine the cornflakes and parsley flakes (if using). Sprinkle cornflake mixture over chicken.

4. Bake, uncovered, in a 350° oven for 18 to 20 minutes or until chicken is tender and no longer pink.

Nutrition Facts per serving: 130 cal.,
1 g total fat (0 g sat. fat), 49 mg chol.,
79 mg sodium, 9 g carbo., 0 g fiber,
20 g pro.
Daily Values: 1% vit. A, 5% vit. C,
1% calcium, 7% iron
Exchanges: ½ Starch, 3 Very Lean Meat

Kickin' Chicken

Barbecue in the winter? Why not—it's all done in the oven. Juicy chicken drumsticks are coated with a slightly sweet barbecue sauce offering a taste of summer while the snow is still flying.

Prep: 20 minutes   Bake: 45 minutes   Oven: 375°F   Makes: 8 servings

Nonstick cooking spray
8 **chicken drumsticks**
¼ **teaspoon salt**
¼ **teaspoon black pepper**
2 **cloves garlic, minced, or 1 teaspoon bottled minced garlic**
2 **teaspoons cooking oil**
¾ **cup bottled barbecue sauce**
¼ **cup catsup**
¼ **cup orange juice or water**
2 **tablespoons packed brown sugar**
2 **tablespoons light molasses or maple-flavored syrup**
Several dashes bottled hot pepper sauce (optional)

1. Lightly coat a 15×10×1-inch baking pan with cooking spray. Skin chicken. Arrange chicken in prepared baking pan. Sprinkle with salt and pepper. Bake in a 375° oven for 25 minutes.

2. Meanwhile, for sauce, in a medium saucepan cook garlic in hot oil over medium heat for 30 seconds. Stir in barbecue sauce, catsup, juice, brown sugar, molasses, and, if desired, hot pepper sauce; heat through.

3. Carefully brush chicken with sauce. Turn chicken and brush with additional sauce. Bake for 20 to 25 minutes more or until chicken is no longer pink (180°F). Reheat any remaining sauce; drizzle some of the sauce over chicken; pass remaining sauce.

Nutrition Facts per serving: 188 cal., 5 g total fat (1 g sat. fat), 78 mg chol., 355 mg sodium, 13 g carbo., 0 g fiber, 22 g pro.
Daily Values: 7% vit. A, 16% vit. C, 3% calcium, 9% iron
Exchanges: 1 Other Carbo., 2½ Lean Meat

Smashed Potato Chicken Potpie

Comfort food was never so easy as this quick-to-fix potpie. It gets a jump-start from purchased mashed potatoes, frozen vegetables, and cooked chicken.

Prep: 30 minutes   Bake: 30 minutes   Stand: 5 minutes   Oven: 375°F
Makes: 6 servings

  3 tablespoons butter or margarine
  ⅓ cup all-purpose flour
  ½ teaspoon seasoned pepper
  ¼ teaspoon salt
  1 14-ounce can reduced-sodium chicken broth
  ¾ cup milk
  2 cups frozen peas and carrots, thawed
  2 cups frozen cut green beans, thawed
  2½ cups chopped cooked chicken or turkey
  1 20-ounce package refrigerated mashed potatoes (about 2⅔ cups)
  2 tablespoons grated Parmesan cheese
  1 clove garlic, minced, or ½ teaspoon bottled minced garlic

1. In a large saucepan melt butter over medium heat. Stir in flour, ¼ teaspoon of the seasoned pepper, and the salt. Add chicken broth and milk all at once. Cook and stir over medium heat until thickened and bubbly. Stir in thawed vegetables and cooked chicken. Pour into an ungreased 3-quart rectangular baking dish.

2. In a medium bowl combine mashed potatoes, cheese, garlic, and the remaining ¼ teaspoon seasoned pepper. Using a spoon, drop potato mixture in large mounds over chicken mixture in baking dish.

3. Bake, uncovered, in a 375° oven for 30 to 40 minutes or until heated through. Let stand for 5 minutes before serving.

Nutrition Facts per serving: 330 cal., 13 g total fat (6 g sat. fat), 72 mg chol., 616 mg sodium, 29 g carbo., 4 g fiber, 25 g pro.
Daily Values: 99% vit. A, 45% vit. C, 11% calcium, 13% iron
Exchanges: 1½ Vegetable, 1 Starch, ½ Other Carbo., 3 Very Lean Meat, 1½ Fat

Chicken Tacos

Take a quick south-of-the-border vacation with these easy-to-make chicken, chile pepper, and tomato stuffed tacos. They're low fat and high flavor—great for family dinners.

Start to Finish: 30 minutes   Makes: 6 servings

    Nonstick cooking spray

½ **cup chopped onion (1 medium)**

1 **clove garlic, minced**

2 **cups chopped cooked chicken**

1 **8-ounce can tomato sauce**

1 **4-ounce can diced green chile peppers, drained**

12 **taco shells**

2 **cups shredded lettuce**

1 **medium tomato, seeded and chopped**

½ **cup finely shredded reduced-fat cheddar cheese and/or Monterey Jack cheese (2 ounces)**

1. Lightly coat a large nonstick skillet with cooking spray. Heat over medium heat. Add the onion and garlic; cook until onion is tender.

2. Stir in the chicken, tomato sauce, and chile peppers. Heat through.

3. Divide chicken mixture among taco shells. Top with lettuce, tomato, and cheese.

Nutrition Facts per serving: 269 cal., 12 g total fat (3 g sat. fat), 48 mg chol., 525 mg sodium, 23 g carbo., 4 g fiber, 19 g pro.
Daily Values: 23% vit. A, 34% vit. C, 14% calcium, 12% iron
Exchanges: 1 Vegetable, 1 Starch, 2 Very Lean Meat, 2 Fat

Saucy Chicken Parmesan

This is one recipe that's sure to become a new family favorite. Kids will love the crispy coated chicken topped with spaghetti sauce and Parmesan cheese.

Prep: *20 minutes*   Bake: *15 minutes*
Oven: *400°F*   Makes: *4 servings*

4 **small skinless, boneless chicken breast halves (about 1 pound)**
  Nonstick cooking spray
1 **slightly beaten egg white**
1 **tablespoon water**
¾ **cup cornflakes, crushed (about ⅓ cup)**
2 **tablespoons grated Parmesan cheese**
¼ **teaspoon dried Italian seasoning, basil, or oregano, crushed**
⅛ **teaspoon black pepper**
1⅓ **cups spaghetti sauce**
4 **ounces dried spaghetti, fettuccine, or other pasta, cooked and drained**
  Grated Parmesan cheese (optional)

1. Place each piece of chicken between 2 pieces of plastic wrap. Pound lightly with the flat side of a meat mallet to flatten slightly (about ½ inch thick). Remove plastic wrap.

2. Lightly coat a shallow baking pan with cooking spray; set aside. In a shallow dish combine egg white and water. In another shallow dish combine crushed cornflakes, the 2 tablespoons Parmesan cheese, Italian seasoning, and pepper. Dip chicken pieces, 1 at a time, into egg mixture; coat with crumb mixture. Place coated chicken pieces in prepared baking pan.

3. Bake in a 400° oven about 15 minutes or until chicken is tender and no longer pink (170°F). Meanwhile, in a small saucepan, warm spaghetti sauce over low heat. Divide pasta among 4 plates. Place chicken on pasta. Spoon spaghetti sauce over chicken. If desired, sprinkle with additional Parmesan cheese.

Nutrition Facts per serving: 312 cal., 3 g total fat (1 g sat. fat), 68 mg chol., 566 mg sodium, 37 g carbo., 3 g fiber, 34 g pro.
Daily Values: 11% vit. A, 12% vit. C, 8% calcium, 23% iron
Exchanges: ½ Vegetable, 1 Starch, 1½ Other Carbo., 4 Very Lean Meat

Chicken and Tortellini Stew

Savory chunks of chicken, thick slices of zucchini, and cheese-filled tortellini mingled in a rich chicken broth make a satisfying stew. Ladle it up for your kids on a chilly fall day.

Start to Finish: 45 minutes   Makes: 6 servings

 2 **cups water**

 1 **14-ounce can chicken broth**

 6 **cups torn spinach**

1½ **cups crinkle-cut or sliced carrots (3 medium)**

 1 **medium zucchini or yellow summer squash, halved lengthwise and cut into ½-inch slices**

 1 **cup dried cheese-filled tortellini**

 1 **red or green sweet pepper, coarsely chopped**

 1 **medium onion, cut into bite-size wedges**

 1 **teaspoon dried basil, crushed**

 ½ **teaspoon dried oregano, crushed**

 ¼ **teaspoon black pepper**

 2 **cups chopped cooked chicken**

1. In a large skillet or Dutch oven combine water and chicken broth. Bring to boiling. Stir in spinach, carrots, zucchini, tortellini, sweet pepper, onion, basil, oregano, and black pepper. Reduce heat. Simmer, covered, about 15 minutes or until the tortellini and vegetables are nearly tender.

2. Stir in cooked chicken. Cook, covered, about 5 minutes more or until tortellini and vegetables are tender.

Nutrition Facts per serving: 210 cal., 6 g total fat (1 g sat. fat), 42 mg chol., 537 mg sodium, 19 g carbo., 3 g fiber, 20 g pro.
Daily Values: 217% vit. A, 75% vit. C, 12% calcium, 12% iron
Exchanges: 1½ Vegetable, 1 Starch, 2 Very Lean Meat, ½ Fat

Creamy Chicken and Rice Soup

You won't have to call your children twice when you serve this creamy chicken soup for dinner. Loaded with carrots, mushrooms and rice, it's a great source of vitamin A, protein, and complex carbohydrates.

Prep: 25 minutes   Cook: 30 minutes   Makes: 6 servings

- ½ cup chopped onion (1 medium)
- ½ cup sliced celery (1 stalk)
- ½ cup sliced carrot or sliced fresh mushrooms
- 1 tablespoon butter or margarine
- 1 14-ounce can reduced-sodium chicken broth
- 1 10¾-ounce can reduced-fat, reduced-sodium condensed cream of chicken soup
- 1 cup water
- 1 6¼-ounce package chicken-flavored rice pilaf mix
- ⅛ teaspoon black pepper
- 2½ cups milk
- 2 cups chopped cooked chicken
- Snipped fresh parsley (optional)

1. In a large saucepan cook onion, celery, and carrot in hot butter over medium heat until tender.

2. Add chicken broth, soup, and water. Stir in pilaf mix with the seasoning packet and pepper. Bring to boiling; reduce heat. Simmer, covered, about 20 minutes or until rice is tender, stirring occasionally.

3. Stir in milk and cooked chicken; heat through. If desired, sprinkle each serving with parsley.

Nutrition Facts per serving: 303 cal., 9 g total fat (4 g sat. fat), 60 mg chol., 979 mg sodium, 34 g carbo., 1 g fiber, 22 g pro.
Daily Values: 59% vit. A, 8% vit. C, 18% calcium, 7% iron
Exchanges: ½ Milk, ½ Vegetable, 1½ Starch, 2 Very Lean Meat, 1 Fat

Turkey Noodle Soup

Kids can't wait to gobble up this turkey and noodle soup. It's spiked with lemon for a refreshing lift to a classic, well-loved recipe.

Prep: 20 minutes   Cook: 26 minutes   Makes: 5 servings (9½ cups)

- 3 cups reduced-sodium chicken broth
- 2¼ cups water
- 1½ cups chopped cooked turkey or chicken
- 1 cup thinly sliced carrots (2 medium)
- 1 medium onion, cut into thin wedges
- ½ cup thinly sliced celery (1 stalk)
- 2 teaspoons snipped fresh thyme or 1 teaspoon dried thyme, crushed
- 2 cups dried wide noodles
- 1 medium yellow summer squash, quartered lengthwise and sliced (1⅓ cups)
- 2 tablespoons lemon juice

1. In a large saucepan combine chicken broth, water, turkey, carrots, onion, celery, and dried thyme (if using). Bring to boiling; reduce heat. Simmer, covered, for 15 minutes.

2. Stir in the noodles and squash. Cook, uncovered, for 10 to 12 minutes or until noodles are tender. Stir in lemon juice and fresh thyme (if using). Cook, uncovered, for 1 minute more.

Nutrition Facts per serving: 163 cal., 3 g total fat (1 g sat. fat), 46 mg chol., 424 mg sodium, 17 g carbo., 2 g fiber, 17 g pro.
Daily Values: 125% vit. A, 16% vit. C, 4% calcium, 10% iron
Exchanges: 1 Vegetable, 1 Starch, 2 Very Lean Meat

Hot Ham and Cheese Turnovers

These golden turnovers hold a surprise for your children—tender ham chunks, broccoli trees, and savory cheddar cheese hide inside.

Prep: 30 minutes   Bake: 13 minutes   Oven: 400°F   Makes: 9 turnovers

> 1¼ **cups chopped cooked ham or turkey breast**
> 1 **cup small broccoli florets**
> ¾ **cup shredded cheddar cheese (3 ounces)**
> 1 **10-ounce package refrigerated pizza dough**
> 1 **tablespoon milk**

1. For filling, in a medium bowl combine ham, broccoli, and cheese; toss to mix. Line a baking sheet with foil; lightly grease foil. Set aside.

2. On a lightly floured surface unroll pizza dough. Roll dough into a 12-inch square. Using a sharp knife, cut into nine 4-inch squares. Spoon about ⅓ cup filling onto each of the squares. Moisten edges of dough with water. Fold dough over filling. Press edges of dough with tines of a fork to seal. Use the fork to prick holes in the top of each turnover to allow steam to escape. Place turnovers on baking sheet. Brush with milk.

3. Bake in a 400° oven for 13 to 15 minutes or until golden. Serve warm.

Nutrition Facts per turnover: 141 cal., 6 g total fat (3 g sat. fat), 21 mg chol., 410 mg sodium, 13 g carbo., 1 g fiber, 8 g pro. *Daily Values:* 5% vit. A, 15% vit. C, 8% calcium, 6% iron *Exchanges:* 1 Starch, 1 Medium-Fat Meat

Team Favorite Turkey Burger

Make lots of these burgers—you're going to need them after the big game. Hungry athletes make these protein-rich turkey burgers disappear in a flash.

Prep: 15 minutes   Broil: 14 minutes   Makes: 4 servings

- ¼ **cup fine dry bread crumbs**
- 3 **tablespoons catsup**
- 4 **teaspoons dill or sweet pickle relish**
- 1 **clove garlic, minced, or ½ teaspoon bottled minced garlic**
- ¼ **teaspoon salt**
- ¼ **teaspoon black pepper**
- 1 **pound uncooked ground turkey or chicken**
- ⅓ **cup low-fat mayonnaise dressing or salad dressing**
- 4 **romaine or green leaf lettuce leaves**
- 8 **tomato slices**
- 4 **whole wheat hamburger buns, split and toasted**

1. Preheat broiler. In a large bowl combine bread crumbs, 2 tablespoons of the catsup, 2 teaspoons of the relish, garlic, salt, and ⅛ teaspoon of the pepper. Add ground turkey; mix well. Shape turkey mixture into four ¾-inch-thick patties.

2. In a small bowl combine mayonnaise dressing, remaining 1 tablespoon catsup, remaining 2 teaspoons relish, and remaining ⅛ teaspoon pepper; set aside.

3. Place patties on the unheated rack of a broiler pan. Broil 4 to 5 inches from the heat for 14 to 18 minutes or until no longer pink (165°F), turning once halfway through broiling.

4. To serve, place lettuce leaves and tomato slices on the bottom halves of buns. Top with burgers. Spoon mayonnaise mixture on burgers. Add top halves of buns.

Nutrition Facts per serving: 343 cal., 12 g total fat (3 g sat. fat), 74 mg chol., 953 mg sodium, 33 g carbo., 3 g fiber, 29 g pro.
Daily Values: 18% vit. A, 16% vit. C, 12% calcium, 21% iron
Exchanges: ½ Vegetable, 2 Starch, 2½ Medium-Fat Meat

Seaside Fish Fingers

A crispy coating flavored with ranch salad dressing seasons these baked fish sticks. The creamy dip provides even more ranch dressing—a taste loved by kids.

Prep: 25 minutes Bake: 10 minutes
Oven: 450°F Makes: 6 servings

1½ **pounds fresh or frozen cod or other fish fillets, about 1 inch thick**

Nonstick cooking spray

⅔ **cup milk**

⅔ **cup all-purpose flour**

1 **cup fine dry bread crumbs**

1 **1-ounce envelope ranch dry salad dressing mix**

½ **teaspoon dry mustard**

¼ **teaspoon black pepper**

¼ **cup butter or margarine, melted**

⅓ **cup light dairy sour cream**

⅓ **cup low-fat mayonnaise dressing or salad dressing**

2 **to 3 tablespoons milk**

1. Thaw fish, if frozen. Rinse fish; pat dry with paper towels. Cut fish into 3×1-inch strips. Lightly coat a baking sheet with cooking spray. Set aside.

2. Place the ⅔ cup milk in a shallow dish. Place flour in another shallow dish. In a third shallow dish combine bread crumbs, 2 tablespoons of the salad dressing mix, ¼ teaspoon of the dry mustard, and the pepper. Add melted butter; stir until combined (if necessary, use your fingers to break up any clumps).

3. Dip fish in the ⅔ cup milk; lightly coat with flour. Dip again in the milk; lightly coat with bread crumb mixture. Place fish on prepared baking sheet. Bake, uncovered, in a 450° oven for 10 to 12 minutes or until fish flakes easily when tested with a fork.

4. Meanwhile, for dipping sauce, in a small bowl combine sour cream, mayonnaise dressing, 2 tablespoons milk, remaining salad dressing mix, and remaining ¼ teaspoon dry mustard. Add additional milk, if necessary, to reach desired consistency. Serve sauce with fish.

Nutrition Facts per serving: 355 cal., 12 g total fat (6 g sat. fat), 80 mg chol., 762 mg sodium, 32 g carbo., 1 g fiber, 26 g pro.
Daily Values: 11% vit. A, 3% vit. C, 12% calcium, 13% iron
Exchanges: 1 Starch, 1 Other Carbo., 3 Very Lean Meat, 2 Fat

Zippity-Doo-Dah Shrimp Sticks

My, oh my, what a wonderful day your kids will have when you serve these sweetly seasoned pineapple and shrimp kabobs for dinner.

Prep: 20 minutes Broil: 7 minutes Makes: 4 servings

12 **ounces fresh or frozen medium shrimp, peeled and deveined**
   Nonstick cooking spray
½ **of a small peeled, cored, fresh pineapple, sliced ½ inch thick**
½ **teaspoon lemon-pepper seasoning**
3 **tablespoons poppy seed salad dressing**
1 **tablespoon pineapple juice or orange juice**
   Fresh pineapple wedges (optional)

1. Thaw shrimp, if frozen. Rinse shrimp; pat dry with paper towels. Lightly coat the unheated rack of a broiler pan with cooking spray; set aside. Preheat broiler.

2. Cut pineapple slices into quarters. Alternately thread shrimp and pineapple onto 8 short or 4 long metal skewers. Transfer skewers to prepared broiler pan. Sprinkle with lemon-pepper seasoning.

3. For brushing sauce, in a small bowl stir together the dressing and juice; set aside.

4. Broil skewers 3 to 4 inches from the heat for 4 minutes. Brush generously with brushing sauce. Carefully turn skewers over. Brush generously with remaining brushing sauce. Broil for 3 to 4 minutes more or until shrimp are opaque and pineapple is heated through. If desired, serve with fresh pineapple wedges.

Nutrition Facts per serving: 160 cal., 5 g total fat (1 g sat. fat), 97 mg chol., 253 mg sodium, 15 g carbo., 1 g fiber, 13 g pro.
Daily Values: 2% vit. A, 21% vit. C, 5% calcium, 9% iron
Exchanges: 1 Fruit, 2 Very Lean Meat, 1 Fat

Fiesta Ziesta Cheese Tostados

Zesty picante sauce livens up these no-meat tostados topped with fiber-rich beans and corn. Teach your kids healthy eating habits by including plenty of high-fiber foods in their diets.

Start to Finish: 30 minutes *Oven:* 400°F *Makes:* 6 servings

  6 6- to 7-inch corn tortillas
  2 teaspoons canola or olive oil
  1 cup vegetarian refried beans
  ⅓ cup picante sauce or salsa
  1 medium red, yellow, or green sweet pepper, cut into thin
     bite-size strips
  ⅓ cup frozen whole kernel corn, thawed and drained
  ¾ cup shredded reduced-fat cheddar cheese (3 ounces)
  1 cup shredded lettuce
     Light dairy sour cream (optional)
     Chopped tomato (optional)

1. Place tortillas in a single layer on an extra-large ungreased baking sheet. Brush top side of each tortilla with a little oil. Bake, uncovered, in a 400° oven for 5 minutes. Remove from oven.

2. Meanwhile, in a small bowl stir together beans and picante sauce. Spread bean mixture evenly over the tortillas. Top with sweet pepper strips and corn. Sprinkle with cheese.

3. Bake for 7 to 8 minutes more or until cheese is melted and filling is heated through. Top with lettuce. If desired, garnish with sour cream and chopped tomato.

Nutrition Facts per serving: 168 cal., 6 g total fat (2 g sat. fat), 10 mg chol., 440 mg sodium, 22 g carbo., 4 g fiber, 8 g pro.
Daily Values: 32% vit. A, 68% vit. C, 17% calcium, 7% iron
Exchanges: ½ Vegetable, 1½ Starch, ½ Lean Meat, ½ Fat

More-Cheese-Please Calzones

Thanks to reduced-fat products, health-conscious diners can indulge in these cheese-stuffed Italian turnovers. Plan ahead and thaw the dough overnight in your refrigerator.

Prep: 50 minutes   Bake: 18 minutes
Oven: 375°F   Makes: 8 servings

Nonstick cooking spray
1 16-ounce loaf frozen bread dough, thawed
½ cup chopped onion (1 medium)
½ cup shredded carrot (1 medium)
½ cup shredded zucchini
2 cloves garlic, minced
1 beaten egg
1 cup light ricotta cheese
1 cup shredded mozzarella cheese (4 ounces)
¼ cup grated Parmesan cheese
1 teaspoon dried Italian seasoning, crushed
1 cup pizza or pasta sauce

1. Coat a very large baking sheet with cooking spray; set aside. Divide bread dough into 8 pieces. Place dough on lightly floured surface; cover with a towel. Let rest while preparing filling.

2. For filling, in a small saucepan cook onion, carrot, zucchini, and garlic, covered, in a small amount of boiling water for 3 minutes. Drain. In a medium bowl stir together egg, ricotta cheese, mozzarella cheese, and Parmesan cheese. Add onion mixture and Italian seasoning.

3. Roll each piece of dough into a 6-inch circle. (If dough seems too elastic, let rest a few minutes; keep remaining dough circles covered.) Spread ⅓ cup filling over each circle, spreading to within ½ inch of edge. Moisten edges with water. Fold each circle in half; seal edge with tines of a fork. Prick with fork; place calzones on prepared baking sheet. Brush with water and, if desired, sprinkle with additional Parmesan. Bake in 375° oven 18 to 20 minutes or until golden. Meanwhile, in a small saucepan heat pizza sauce; serve with calzones.

Nutrition Facts per serving: 264 cal., 7 g total fat (3 g sat. fat), 43 mg chol., 503 mg sodium, 34 g carbo., 2 g fiber, 16 g pro.
Daily Values: 45% vit. A, 8% vit. C, 36% calcium, 14% iron
Exchanges: ½ Vegetable, 2 Starch, 1½ Lean Meat, ½ Fat

Triple-Decker Tortilla

Twenty minutes is all it takes to build a healthful family dinner. Salsa, corn, beans, and cheese separate layers of tortillas in this tasty hot Tex-Mex casserole.

Start to Finish: 20 minutes   Oven: 450°F   Makes: 4 servings

Nonstick cooking spray
1 **cup canned pinto beans, rinsed and drained**
1 **cup salsa**
4 **6-inch corn tortillas**
½ **cup frozen whole kernel corn**
½ **cup shredded reduced-fat Monterey Jack or cheddar cheese (2 ounces)**
½ **cup shredded lettuce**

1. Lightly coat a 9-inch pie plate with cooking spray; set aside. Place beans in a small bowl; slightly mash the beans. In a small saucepan or skillet cook and stir beans over medium heat for 2 to 3 minutes. Set aside.

2. Spoon ¼ cup of the salsa into bottom of prepared pie plate. Top with 1 of the tortillas. Layer half of the mashed beans, 1 tortilla, corn, ¼ cup of the cheese, ¼ cup salsa, 1 tortilla, remaining bean mixture, remaining tortilla, and remaining ½ cup salsa.

3. Cover with foil; bake in a 450° oven for 12 minutes. (Or cover with microwave-safe plastic wrap; microwave on 100 percent power [high] for 4 minutes, rotating once.) Remove foil. Sprinkle with remaining ¼ cup cheese.

4. Bake, uncovered, 3 minutes more. (Or microwave on high for 30 seconds more.) Top with shredded lettuce.

Nutrition Facts per serving: 219 cal., 5 g total fat (2 g sat. fat), 10 mg chol., 813 mg sodium, 38 g carbo., 6 g fiber, 10 g pro.
Daily Values: 12% vit. A, 18% vit. C, 19% calcium, 8% iron
Exchanges: ½ Vegetable, 2 Starch, ½ Lean Meat, ½ Fat

Mighty Mac and Cheese

Tried and true macaroni and cheese can't be beat when it's low in fat. This calcium-packed entrée contains 70 percent less fat than the traditional version.

Prep: 30 minutes   Bake: 25 minutes   Stand: 5 minutes   Oven: 350°F   Makes: 4 servings

1⅓ **cups dried corkscrew pasta or elbow macaroni (about 5 ounces)**
 ¼ **cup nonfat dry milk powder**
 ¼ **cup finely chopped onion**
 2 **tablespoons all-purpose flour**
 ¼ **teaspoon salt**
1½ **cups milk**
 10 **slices reduced-fat American cheese (7 ounces), torn**
 6 **flavored crisp breadsticks, such as cheese or garlic, coarsely crushed (1 ounce total)**

1. Cook pasta according to package directions. Drain; set aside.

2. Meanwhile, in a medium saucepan stir together the milk powder, onion, flour, and salt. Gradually stir in the milk until mixture is smooth. Cook and stir over medium heat until thickened and bubbly. Reduce heat to low. Add the cheese, stirring until melted. Stir in the pasta. Spoon mixture into a 1½-quart casserole.

3. Bake, uncovered, in a 350° oven about 25 minutes or until bubbly, stirring once and topping with crushed breadsticks after 15 minutes. Let stand 5 minutes before serving.

Nutrition Facts per serving: 344 cal., 10 g total fat (5 g sat. fat), 33 mg chol., 889 mg sodium, 44 g carbo., 1 g fiber, 20 g pro.
Daily Values: 21% vit. A, 3% vit. C, 67% calcium, 8% iron
Exchanges: ½ Milk, 2 ½ Starch, 1½ Lean Meat, ½ Fat

Pasta Pizza

It's pasta! It's pizza! No, it's a super casserole sure to satisfy little and big appetites. Multicolored pasta forms a crust for the Italian-seasoned tomato, mushroom, pepperoni, and cheese toppings.

Prep: 25 minutes Bake: 30 minutes
Oven: 350°F Makes: 6 servings

Nonstick cooking spray
5 **ounces packaged dried tricolored or plain corkscrew pasta (2 cups)**
2 **slightly beaten eggs**
½ **cup milk**
1 **cup shredded 4-cheese pizza cheese (4 ounces)**
¾ **cup chopped sweet pepper and/or chopped zucchini**
1 **14½-ounce can Italian-style stewed tomatoes, undrained**
½ **teaspoon dried Italian seasoning, crushed**
1 **4½-ounce jar sliced mushrooms, drained (optional)**
½ **of a 6-ounce package sliced turkey pepperoni**
2 **tablespoons grated Parmesan cheese**

1. Lightly coat a 12-inch pizza pan (with sides) with cooking spray; set aside. Cook pasta according to package directions. Drain pasta; rinse with cold water. Drain again.

2. For pasta crust, in a large bowl combine eggs, milk, and ½ cup of the pizza cheese. Stir in pasta. Spread pasta mixture evenly in prepared pan. Bake in a 350° oven for 20 minutes.

3. Meanwhile, coat a large skillet with cooking spray. Heat over medium heat. Add sweet pepper and cook until crisp-tender. Add undrained tomatoes and Italian seasoning. Bring to boiling; reduce heat. Simmer, uncovered, for 10 minutes or until most of the liquid is evaporated, stirring occasionally. If desired, stir in mushrooms.

4. Arrange pepperoni over the pasta crust. Spoon tomato mixture over pepperoni. Sprinkle with ½ cup remaining pizza cheese and the Parmesan cheese. Bake for 10 to 12 minutes more or until heated through and cheese is melted. To serve, cut into wedges.

Nutrition Facts per serving: 242 cal., 6 g total fat (2 g sat. fat), 96 mg chol., 574 mg sodium, 31 g carbo., 2 g fiber, 14 g pro.
Daily Values: 27% vit. A, 61% vit. C, 12% calcium, 11% iron
Exchanges: 1 Vegetable, 1½ Starch, 1½ Lean Meat

Tater Soup

Potato soup never tasted so good as this version that bursts with vegetables. It makes a fabulous cold-weather dinner and provides lots of vitamin A, vitamin C, complex carbohydrates, and fiber.

Prep: 25 minutes   Cook: 15 minutes   Makes: 4 to 6 servings (about 6 cups)

4 medium round red, white, or yellow potatoes, cut into bite-size pieces (about 1¼ pounds)
½ cup sliced carrot (1 medium)
½ cup sliced celery (1 stalk)
2 tablespoons butter or margarine
2 tablespoons all-purpose flour
½ teaspoon salt
⅛ teaspoon ground white pepper
1½ cups milk
1 14-ounce can reduced-sodium chicken broth
Shredded reduced-fat cheddar cheese (optional)

1. In a large saucepan cook unpeeled potatoes in a large amount of boiling salted water for 5 minutes. Add carrot and celery. Cook about 10 minutes more or until vegetables are tender; drain. Transfer 1 cup of the vegetable mixture to a small bowl; set remaining vegetable mixture aside. Use a potato masher to mash the 1 cup vegetables until nearly smooth. Set mashed vegetable mixture aside.

2. In the same saucepan melt butter. Stir in flour, salt, and pepper. Add milk all at once. Cook and stir until slightly thickened and bubbly.

3. Stir in the reserved cooked vegetables, mashed vegetable mixture, and broth. Cook and stir over medium heat until heated through. If necessary, stir in additional milk to reach desired consistency. Season to taste with additional salt and ground white pepper. If desired, sprinkle with shredded cheese.

Nutrition Facts per serving: 234 cal., 8 g total fat (5 g sat. fat), 24 mg chol., 698 mg sodium, 33 g carbo., 3 g fiber, 8 g pro.
Daily Values: 86% vit. A, 40% vit. C, 14% calcium, 13% iron
Exchanges: ½ Milk, ½ Vegetable, 1½ Starch, 1 Fat

Macaroni and Cheese Chowder

Start with a package of macaroni and cheese, then add ham and cream-style corn for a speedy dinner sure to satisfy hungry kids. It's high in complex carbohydrates for energy and protein for growth.

Start to Finish: 25 minutes   *Makes:* 4 servings

> 1 14-ounce can reduced-sodium chicken broth
> 1 cup water
> 1 5½-ounce package macaroni and cheese dinner mix
> 1 14¾-ounce can cream-style corn
> 1 cup chopped cooked ham (5 ounces)
> ½ cup milk

1. In a large saucepan bring chicken broth and water to boiling. Gradually add macaroni from mix. Reduce heat to medium-low. Simmer, covered, for 11 to 14 minutes or until macaroni is tender.

2. Stir in cream-style corn, ham, milk, and contents of cheese packet. Cook and stir over medium heat until heated through.

Nutrition Facts per serving: 301 cal., 6 g total fat (2 g sat. fat), 27 mg chol., 1,324 mg sodium, 48 g carbo., 2 g fiber, 16 g pro.
Daily Values: 3% vit. A, 9% vit. C, 10% calcium, 12% iron
Exchanges: 2½ Starch, ½ Other Carbo., 1½ Lean Meat

MOM SAYS, "EAT YOUR VEGETABLES"

Imagine your children eating vegetables without any prodding! That's what will happen when you fix Easy Cheesy Broccoli and Rice, Parmesan Potato Coins, or any of these veggie delights.

6

Burst-of-Orange Butternut Squash

Ginger-Honey Glazed Carrots

Sweet honey blends with pungent ginger glazing these tender young carrots. Rich in vitamin A, carrots boost immunity, improve night vision, and supply fiber.

Prep: 15 minutes   *Cook:* 15 minutes   *Makes:* 10 to 12 servings

- 6 **cups water**
- ¾ **teaspoon salt**
- 3 **pounds packaged peeled baby carrots**
- 2 **tablespoons butter or margarine**
- 2 **tablespoons honey**
- 4 **teaspoons minced fresh ginger**

1. Line a baking sheet with paper towels. In a 12- or 14-inch heavy skillet combine water and salt. Bring to boiling over high heat. Add carrots. Return to boiling; reduce heat. Simmer, covered, for 10 to 12 minutes or just until carrots are tender. Drain carrots. Turn carrots out onto prepared baking sheet. Pat dry with additional paper towels.

2. To glaze carrots, in the same heavy skillet combine butter, honey, and fresh ginger. Stir constantly over medium heat until butter is melted. Carefully add the carrots. Toss gently for 2 to 3 minutes or until carrots are thoroughly coated with glaze and heated through.

3. To serve, arrange carrots in a shallow bowl or on a platter; drizzle carrots with remaining glaze from the pan.

Make-Ahead Tip: Carrots may be cooked, cooled, covered, and refrigerated up to one day ahead. Bring to room temperature (takes about 1 hour) when ready to glaze. Heat carrots in glaze for 4 to 5 minutes.

Nutrition Facts per serving: 87 cal., 3 g total fat (2 g sat. fat), 7 mg chol., 131 mg sodium, 15 g carbo., 2 g fiber, 1 g pro.
Daily Values: 369% vit. A, 14% vit. C, 3% calcium, 6% iron
Exchanges: 2½ Vegetable, ½ Fat

Teriyaki Green Beans with Carrots

Toasty sesame seeds and savory teriyaki sauce top two of kids' favorite vegetables—green beans and carrots. Serve it for dinner tonight.

Start to Finish: 30 minutes   Makes: 6 to 8 servings

- 1 pound green beans, cut into 1-inch pieces (4 cups)
- 3 medium carrots, cut into bite-size strips (2 cups)
- 1 tablespoon butter or margarine
- 1 teaspoon cornstarch
- 3 tablespoons reduced-sodium teriyaki sauce
- 1 tablespoon water
- 1 teaspoon sesame seeds, toasted (optional)

1. In a medium saucepan cook green beans, covered, in a small amount of boiling salted water about 10 minutes or until crisp-tender, adding carrots the last 5 minutes of cooking. Drain; set vegetables aside.

2. In the same saucepan melt butter; stir in cornstarch. Add the teriyaki sauce and water. Cook and stir until thickened and bubbly. Return vegetables to saucepan; toss gently to coat. Heat through. If desired, sprinkle each serving with sesame seeds.

Nutrition Facts per serving: 59 cal., 2 g total fat (1 g sat. fat), 5 mg chol., 158 mg sodium, 9 g carbo., 3 g fiber, 2 g pro.
Daily Values: 180% vit. A, 18% vit. C, 3% calcium, 5% iron
Exchanges: 1 1/2 Vegetable, 1/2 Fat

Italian Veggie Dunkers

Better make lots of these crispy-coated vegetables. Kids love dipping them in pizza sauce and munching them down.

Prep: 25 minutes   *Bake:* 20 minutes
Oven: 400°F   *Makes:* 6 servings

Nonstick cooking spray
⅔ **cup seasoned fine dry bread crumbs**
2 **tablespoons grated Parmesan cheese**
⅛ **teaspoon salt**
2 **slightly beaten egg whites**
1 **tablespoon milk**
4 **cups cauliflower florets and/or broccoli florets**
2 **tablespoons butter or margarine, melted**
1 **15-ounce can pizza sauce**

1. Lightly coat a 15×10×1-inch baking pan with cooking spray; set aside. In a large plastic bag combine bread crumbs, cheese, and salt. In another large plastic bag combine egg whites and milk.

2. Add the vegetables to the plastic bag with the egg mixture. Close bag and shake to coat well. Add vegetables to plastic bag with crumb mixture. Close bag and shake to coat well. Place coated vegetables on the prepared baking pan. Drizzle melted butter over vegetables.

3. Bake in a 400° oven about 20 minutes or until golden brown, stirring twice. Meanwhile, heat the pizza sauce in a small saucepan over medium heat. Serve vegetables with warm pizza sauce.

Nutrition Facts per serving: 144 cal., 6 g total fat (3 g sat. fat), 13 mg chol., 543 mg sodium, 18 g carbo., 3 g fiber, 7 g pro.
Daily Values: 26% vit. A, 72% vit. C, 9% calcium, 9% iron
Exchanges: 2 Vegetable, ½ Starch, 1 Fat

Easy Cheesy Broccoli and Rice

This cheesy rice and broccoli casserole convinces even the pickiest eaters that broccoli tastes good! It's a great source of antioxidant vitamins A and C and provides calcium for healthy bones.

Start to Finish: 15 minutes *Makes:* 6 servings

- 1 10-ounce package frozen chopped broccoli
- 1 cup quick-cooking rice
- 1 cup water
- ¼ teaspoon salt
- 1 cup shredded reduced-fat cheddar or Swiss cheese (4 ounces)

1. In a medium saucepan combine frozen broccoli, uncooked rice, water, and salt. Bring to boiling, stirring frequently to break up frozen broccoli.

2. Remove from heat. Cover and let stand for 5 minutes. Return saucepan to burner. Over low heat, add cheese, stirring just until cheese is melted. If desired, serve in bowls and sprinkle with additional shredded reduced-fat cheddar cheese.

Nutrition Facts per serving: 132 cal., 4 g total fat (3 g sat. fat), 13 mg chol., 270 mg sodium, 16 g carbo., 1 g fiber, 7 g pro.
Daily Values: 24% vit. A, 44% vit. C, 16% calcium, 6% iron
Exchanges: ½ Vegetable, 1 Starch, ½ Medium-Fat Meat

Oven-Roasted Vegetables

A little olive oil and your children's favorite herb add zest to oven-roasted sweet potatoes, carrots, parsnips, and red onions. This flavorful combination supplies abundant vitamin A to protect against infections and promote the growth and health of body tissues.

Prep: 15 minutes   Roast: 35 minutes   Oven: 425°F   Makes: 6 servings

- 2 medium sweet potatoes and/or white potatoes, peeled and cut into 1-inch cubes
- 1 cup peeled baby carrots or 2 carrots, cut into 1-inch pieces
- 1 medium parsnip, peeled and cut into 1-inch pieces
- 1 medium red onion, cut into thin wedges (optional)
- 1 tablespoon olive oil
- 3 cloves garlic, minced
- 1 teaspoon dried mixed herbs (such as marjoram, thyme, rosemary, and oregano), crushed
- ¼ teaspoon salt
- ⅛ teaspoon black pepper

1. In a 13×9×2-inch baking pan arrange potatoes, carrots, parsnip, and, if desired, red onion. In a small bowl combine oil, garlic, mixed herbs, salt, and pepper. Drizzle oil mixture over vegetables; toss to coat. Cover with foil.

2. Bake in a 425° oven for 30 minutes. Remove foil; stir vegetables. Bake, uncovered, for 5 to 10 minutes more or until vegetables are tender.

Nutrition Facts per serving: 83 cal., 2 g total fat (0 g sat. fat), 0 mg chol., 110 mg sodium, 15 g carbo., 3 g fiber, 1 g pro.
Daily Values: 269% vit. A, 23% vit. C, 3% calcium, 3% iron
Exchanges: 1 Vegetable, ½ Starch, ½ Fat

Cheddar Scalloped Potatoes

A layer of reduced-fat cheddar cheese hidden in the middle turns ordinary potatoes into a kid-pleasing casserole.

Prep: 35 minutes *Bake:* 70 minutes *Stand:* 10 minutes
Oven: 350°F *Makes:* 8 to 10 servings

Nonstick cooking spray
½ cup finely chopped onion (1 medium)
1 clove garlic, minced
2 tablespoons butter or margarine
¼ cup all-purpose flour
¾ teaspoon salt
¼ teaspoon black pepper
2 cups milk
6 medium potatoes (2 pounds)
1 cup shredded reduced-fat sharp cheddar cheese (4 ounces)

1. Lightly coat a 2-quart square baking dish with cooking spray; set aside. For sauce, in a medium saucepan cook onion and garlic in hot butter over medium heat until tender but not brown. Stir in flour, salt, and pepper. Add milk all at once. (If necessary, stir with a whisk until smooth.) Cook and stir over medium heat until thickened and bubbly. Remove saucepan from heat.

2. Peel and thinly slice the potatoes. Layer half (about 3 cups) of the potatoes in prepared baking dish. Cover with half (about 1 cup) of the sauce. Sprinkle with all of the cheese. Top with remaining potatoes. Pour remaining sauce over all. Cover with foil.

3. Bake, covered, in a 350° oven for 45 minutes. Remove foil. Bake, uncovered, about 25 minutes more or until potatoes are tender. Let stand 10 minutes before serving.

Nutrition Facts per serving: 187 cal., 7 g total fat (5 g sat. fat), 23 mg chol., 405 mg sodium, 22 g carbo., 2 g fiber, 8 g pro.
Daily Values: 8% vit. A, 24% vit. C, 18% calcium, 5% iron
Exchanges: 1½ Starch, ½ Medium-Fat Meat, ½ Fat

Veggie Mash

Adding cauliflower and carrot to classic, kid-favorite mashed potatoes fortifies them with extra vitamin A, vitamin C, and folate.

Start to Finish: **30 minutes**   *Makes:* **6 servings**

> 3 **medium baking potatoes (1 pound), peeled and cubed**
> 1 **cup coarsely chopped cauliflower**
> ½ **cup sliced carrot or coarsely chopped cauliflower**
> ¼ **cup light dairy sour cream**
> ¼ **teaspoon salt**
> 2 **tablespoons finely shredded Parmesan cheese**

1. In a medium saucepan cook potatoes, cauliflower, and carrot, covered, in enough boiling salted water to cover for 15 to 20 minutes or until tender. Drain. Mash with a potato masher or beat with an electric mixer on low speed. Add sour cream and salt. Mash or beat until combined. Season to taste with additional salt and black pepper. Top each serving with Parmesan cheese.

Nutrition Facts per serving: 113 cal., 4 g total fat (2 g sat. fat), 11 mg chol., 303 mg sodium, 13 g carbo., 2 g fiber, 6 g pro.
Daily Values: 54% vit. A, 25% vit. C, 17% calcium, 3% iron
Exchanges: 1 Vegetable, ½ Starch, 1 Fat

Oven-Fried Onion Rings

Become a dinnertime hero—serve these crispy, crumb-coated onion rings. They're oven-fried and contain only 15 percent of the fat found in the traditional deep-fat fried recipe.

Prep: 25 minutes   Bake: 12 minutes   Oven: 450°F   Makes: 6 servings

Nonstick cooking spray
¾ **cup fine dry bread crumbs**
3 **tablespoons butter or margarine, melted**
¼ **teaspoon salt**
2 **medium sweet yellow or white onions, cut into ¼-inch slices and separated into rings**
2 **slightly beaten egg whites**

1. Lightly coat a very large baking sheet with cooking spray. In a small bowl stir together bread crumbs, melted butter, and salt. Spread about one-fourth of the crumb mixture on a sheet of waxed paper.

2. Using a fork, dip the onion rings in the egg whites, then in the bread crumb mixture. Replace waxed paper and add more of the crumb mixture as needed.* Arrange the coated onion rings in a single layer on the prepared baking sheet.

3. Bake in a 450° oven for 12 to 15 minutes or until the onions are tender and the coating is crisp and golden.

*Note: The crumb mixture will not stick if combined with egg white mixture. Use one-fourth of the crumb mixture at a time.

Nutrition Facts per serving: 128 cal., 7 g total fat (4 g sat. fat), 16 mg chol., 283 mg sodium, 13 g carbo., 1 g fiber, 4 g pro.
Daily Values: 5% vit. A, 3% vit. C, 3% calcium, 5% iron
Exchanges: 1 Vegetable, ½ Starch, ½ Fat

Parmesan Potato Coins

Kids devour these baked potato rounds topped with aromatic Italian herbs and coated with mouthwatering Parmesan cheese.

Prep: 20 minutes   Bake: 1 hour   Oven: 350°F   Makes: 6 servings

- 6 **medium potatoes (about 2 pounds)**
- ⅓ **cup butter or margarine, melted**
- ¼ **cup all-purpose flour**
- ¼ **cup grated Parmesan cheese**
- ¼ **teaspoon salt**
- ⅛ **teaspoon black pepper**
- ¼ **teaspoon dried Italian seasoning, crushed**

1. Peel potatoes. Cut each potato crosswise into 4 rounds. Pour the melted butter into a 15×10×1-inch baking pan. In a large self-sealing plastic bag combine flour, Parmesan cheese, salt, and pepper. Add several potato rounds to the bag at a time; seal bag. Shake bag to coat potatoes with the flour mixture. Place potato rounds on top of butter in baking pan.

2. Bake, uncovered, in a 350° oven for 30 minutes. Turn potatoes over. Sprinkle with Italian seasoning. Bake about 30 minutes more or until potatoes are tender.

Nutrition Facts per serving: 222 cal., 12 g total fat (7 g sat. fat), 32 mg chol., 290 mg sodium, 25 g carbo., 2 g fiber, 5 g pro.
Daily Values: 9% vit. A, 29% vit. C, 7% calcium, 7% iron
Exchanges: 1½ Starch, 2 Fat

Cook with Your Kids

Looking for a little "buy in" on tonight's dinner? Kids are more willing to try a new healthful dish or ingredient if they play a part in selecting and preparing the meal. So invite your kids into the kitchen, divide the tasks among them (making sure, of course, they are age-appropriate), and get cooking! There will be fewer complaints at the table—guaranteed.

Burst-of-Orange Butternut Squash

A splash of orange juice and a hint of sweet maple syrup add kid-approved flavors to baked butternut squash— a vegetable plentiful in beta-carotene.

Prep: 25 minutes   Roast: 25 minutes   Oven: 425°F   Makes: 4 servings

Nonstick cooking spray

1 **pound butternut squash, peeled, seeded, and cut into $1/2$-inch pieces**

$1/3$ **cup orange juice**

1 **tablespoon maple syrup**

$1/4$ **teaspoon salt**

$1/8$ **teaspoon ground black pepper (optional)**

Dash ground cinnamon

1 **tablespoon butter or margarine**

1. Lightly coat a 2-quart rectangular baking dish with cooking spray. Place squash in prepared baking dish. In a small bowl combine orange juice, maple syrup, salt, pepper (if desired), and cinnamon. Drizzle over squash; toss to coat. Dot with butter.

2. Bake in a 425° oven, uncovered, about 25 minutes or until squash is tender, stirring twice.

Nutrition Facts per serving: 91 cal., 3 g total fat (2 g sat. fat), 8 mg chol., 182 mg sodium, 15 g carbo., 2 g fiber, 2 g pro.
Daily Values: 91% vit. A, 37% vit. C, 4% calcium, 4% iron
Exchanges: 1 Starch, $1/2$ Fat

Gingery Sugar Snap Peas

A light coating of sweet peach preserves, soy sauce, and ginger tempts children to enjoy the pleasures of crisp-tender sugar snap peas.

Start to Finish: 15 minutes   *Makes:* 6 servings

3 cups fresh sugar snap peas or frozen loose-pack sugar snap peas
1 tablespoon butter or margarine
1 tablespoon peach preserves
1 teaspoon soy sauce
Dash ground ginger
Dash black pepper

1. Remove strings and tips from fresh peas. Cook fresh peas in a medium saucepan, covered, in a small amount of boiling salted water for 2 to 4 minutes or until crisp-tender. (Or cook frozen peas according to package directions.) Drain well; set peas aside.

2. In the same saucepan melt butter; stir in preserves, soy sauce, ginger, and pepper. Return peas to saucepan, stirring to coat.

Nutrition Facts per serving: 78 cal., 2 g total fat (1 g sat. fat), 5 mg chol., 85 mg sodium, 11 g carbo., 3 g fiber, 3 g pro.
Daily Values: 2% vit. A, 32% vit. C, 4% calcium, 6% iron
Exchanges: 2 Vegetable, 1/2 Fat

Vegetable Fried Rice

It's necessary to use chilled rice when making this side dish. Make the rice ahead and chill it overnight or use leftover rice.

Start to Finish: 20 minutes   *Makes: 8 side-dish servings*

- 1 **tablespoon toasted sesame oil**
- 2 **teaspoons fresh or bottled minced garlic**
- 2 **teaspoons fresh or bottled minced ginger**
- 3 **cups mixed cut-up fresh vegetables (packaged or from the salad bar), such as sweet peppers, red onion, sliced mushrooms, broccoli florets, or thin baby carrots**
- 1½ **cups coarsely chopped bok choy**
- 3 **cups cold cooked white or brown rice**
- ¼ **cup reduced-sodium soy sauce**
- 2 **tablespoons thinly sliced green onion (1) or snipped fresh cilantro (optional)**

1. In a 12-inch nonstick skillet heat sesame oil over medium heat. Add garlic and ginger; cook and stir for 1 minute. Add mixed vegetables and bok choy; cook and stir for 3 to 4 minutes or until vegetables are crisp-tender. Add rice and soy sauce; cook and stir for 3 minutes. If desired, sprinkle with green onion.

Note: For a main-dish for four, add 2 cups diced cooked chicken or shrimp with the rice and soy sauce.

Nutrition Facts per serving: 114 cal., 2 g total fat (0 g sat. fat), 0 mg chol., 301 mg sodium, 20 g carbo., 1 g fiber, 3 g pro.
Daily Values: 14% vit. A, 48% vit. C, 4% calcium, 7% iron
Exchanges: 1 Vegetable, 1 Starch

Red Tomato Soup

Better than canned, this homemade soup explodes with flavor. Top it with crispy croutons and shredded Parmesan cheese for soup sure to please famished kids.

Prep: 15 minutes   Cook: 15 minutes   Makes: 6 servings (about 4½ cups)

½ **cup chopped carrot (1 medium)**
¼ **cup chopped onion**
¼ **cup chopped celery**
1 **tablespoon butter or margarine**
1 **28-ounce can diced tomatoes, undrained**
1 **5½-ounce can vegetable juice**
2 **teaspoons sugar**
½ **teaspoon dried Italian seasoning, crushed**
¼ **teaspoon salt**
⅛ **teaspoon black pepper**
½ **to 1 cup water**
¾ **cup Italian-style croutons**
¼ **cup finely shredded Parmesan cheese (optional)**

1. In a 2-quart saucepan cook carrot, onion, and celery in hot butter for 5 to 8 minutes or until tender, stirring occasionally. Add undrained tomatoes, vegetable juice, sugar, Italian seasoning, salt, and pepper. Bring to boiling; reduce heat. Simmer, uncovered, for 10 minutes. Remove from heat.

2. If desired, cool slightly. In a blender container or food processor bowl place half of the tomato mixture. Cover and blend or process until smooth. Repeat with remaining tomato mixture. Return all of the soup to the saucepan. Add enough water to reach desired consistency. Heat through.

3. To serve, ladle into bowls. Top with croutons and, if desired, sprinkle with Parmesan cheese.

Nutrition Facts per serving: 107 cal., 4 g total fat (2 g sat. fat), 8 mg chol., 542 mg sodium, 14 g carbo., 2 g fiber, 3 g pro.
Daily Values: 66% vit. A, 43% vit. C, 11% calcium, 6% iron
Exchanges: 2½ Vegetable, 1 Fat

SWEET TREATS

Satisfy your child's sweet tooth with healthy alternatives to packaged desserts. Look for fun-to-eat treats such as Berry Dessert Nachos or Fast and Fruity Tarts along with calorie-trimmed family favorites.

7

Lunch Box Oatmeal Cookies

Chocolate-Cream Cheese Cupcakes

A sprinkle of crunchy granola makes an easy topping for these chocolate cupcakes. Reduced-fat cream cheese keeps the cupcakes moist and low in fat and calories.

Prep: 30 minutes Bake: 25 minutes Oven: 350°F Makes: 18 cupcakes

½ **of an 8-ounce package reduced-fat cream cheese (Neufchâtel), softened**

1⅓ **cups sugar**

¼ **cup refrigerated or frozen egg product, thawed**

⅓ **cup miniature semisweet chocolate pieces**

1½ **cups all-purpose flour**

¼ **cup unsweetened cocoa powder**

1 **teaspoon baking powder**

¼ **teaspoon baking soda**

⅛ **teaspoon salt**

1 **cup water**

⅓ **cup cooking oil**

1 **tablespoon vinegar**

1 **teaspoon vanilla**

½ **cup low-fat granola**

1. Line 18 muffin cups with paper bake cups; set aside.

2. In a small mixing bowl beat cream cheese with an electric mixer on medium speed until smooth. Add ⅓ cup of the sugar and the egg product. Beat on medium speed for 1 minute or until smooth. Stir in the semisweet chocolate pieces; set aside.

3. In a large mixing bowl combine remaining 1 cup sugar, the flour, cocoa powder, baking powder, baking soda, and salt. Add water, oil, vinegar, and vanilla. Beat with an electric mixer on medium speed for 2 minutes, scraping sides of bowl occasionally. Spoon batter into the prepared muffin cups, filling each half full. Spoon about 1 tablespoon of the cream cheese mixture over each. Sprinkle with granola.

4. Bake in a 350° oven for 25 to 30 minutes or until tops spring back when lightly touched. Cool in pan on wire racks for 10 minutes. Remove cupcakes from pan; cool thoroughly on racks.

Nutrition Facts per cupcake: 187 cal., 7 g total fat (2 g sat. fat), 5 mg chol., 95 mg sodium, 28 g carbo., 0 g fiber, 3 g pro.
Daily Values: 2% vit. A, 4% calcium, 7% iron
Exchanges: 2 Other Carbo., 1½ Fat

Dream Cream Puffs

These light and airy puffs are filled with a low-calorie, minty chocolate filling, proving there's plenty of room in a healthful diet for chocolate.

Prep: 25 minutes   Bake: 30 minutes   Cool: 1 hour
Oven: 400°F   Makes: 8 servings

Nonstick cooking spray
½ **cup water**
2 **tablespoons butter or margarine**
½ **cup all-purpose flour**
2 **eggs**
1 **4-serving-size package instant chocolate pudding mix**
   or reduced-calorie regular chocolate pudding mix
2 **cups fat-free milk**
⅛ **teaspoon peppermint extract**
Sifted powdered sugar
Fresh strawberries (optional)

1. Lightly coat a baking sheet with cooking spray; set aside.

2. In a small saucepan combine water and butter. Bring to boiling. Add flour all at once, stirring vigorously. Cook and stir until mixture forms a ball. Remove from heat. Cool for 10 minutes. Add eggs, 1 at a time, beating well with a wooden spoon after each addition. Drop mixture in 8 mounds, 3 inches apart, on the prepared baking sheet.

3. Bake in a 400° oven about 30 minutes or until golden. Transfer cream puffs to a wire rack; cool. Cut tops from cream puffs; remove the soft dough from inside. Cool cream puffs completely on a wire rack.

4. Meanwhile, for filling, prepare pudding mix according to package directions using the fat-free milk. Stir in peppermint extract. Cover surface with plastic wrap. Chill.

5. To serve, spoon about ¼ cup of the filling into the bottom half of each cream puff. Replace tops. Sprinkle with sifted powdered sugar. If desired, garnish with fresh strawberries.

Nutrition Facts per serving: 146 cal., 4 g total fat (2 g sat. fat), 63 mg chol., 284 mg sodium, 22 g carbo., 0 g fiber, 4 g pro.
Daily Values: 6% vit. A, 1% vit. C, 8% calcium, 4% iron
Exchanges: 1½ Other Carbo., ½ Fat

Brownie-Fruit Pizza

Here's one way to convince your kids to eat fresh fruit. A delectable brownie crust and a drizzle of chocolate syrup make kiwifruit, peaches, nectarines, or berries irresistible.

Prep: 15 minutes   Bake: 20 minutes   Cool: 1 hour   Oven: 350°F   Makes: 12 servings

Nonstick cooking spray

½ **cup sugar**

3 **tablespoons butter or margarine, softened**

¼ **cup refrigerated or frozen egg product, thawed**

¾ **cup chocolate-flavored syrup**

⅔ **cup all-purpose flour**

3 **cups assorted fruit such as sliced, peeled kiwifruit; mandarin orange sections; sliced bananas; sliced, peeled peaches; sliced nectarines; strawberries; raspberries; and/or blueberries**

½ **cup chocolate-flavored syrup**

1. Lightly coat a 12-inch pizza pan with cooking spray. Set aside.

2. For crust, in a medium mixing bowl combine sugar and butter. Beat with an electric mixer on medium speed until creamy. Add the egg product; beat well. Alternately add the ¾ cup chocolate-flavored syrup and the flour, beating after each addition on low speed until combined. Spread into the prepared pizza pan.

3. Bake in a 350° oven about 20 minutes or until top springs back when lightly touched. Cool on a wire rack.

4. To serve, cut the brownie into 12 wedges. Top each wedge with fruit; drizzle with the ½ cup chocolate-flavored syrup.

148

Nutrition Facts per serving: 187 cal., 3 g total fat (2 g sat. fat), 8 mg chol., 61 mg sodium, 39 g carbo., 2 g fiber, 2 g pro.
Daily Values: 5% vit. A, 37% vit. C, 1% calcium, 5% iron
Exchanges: ½ Fruit, 2 Other Carbo., ½ Fat

Strawberry Shortcake

Strawberries are one of nature's nutritional powerhouses—they overflow with vitamin C, soluble fiber, and anthocyanins. Serve them in a calorie-trimmed version of this time-honored dessert that's been a favorite with generations of kids.

Prep: 20 minutes   Chill: 1 hour   Bake: 7 minutes
Oven: 450°F   Makes: 8 servings

- 3 **cups sliced fresh strawberries**
- 2 **tablespoons sugar**
- 1⅔ **cups all-purpose flour**
- 1 **tablespoon sugar**
- 2 **teaspoons baking powder**
- ¼ **teaspoon baking soda**
- 3 **tablespoons butter or margarine**
- 1 **beaten egg**
- ½ **cup buttermilk**
- 2 **cups frozen light whipped dessert topping, thawed, or one 1.3-ounce envelope whipped dessert topping mix**

1. In a medium bowl stir together strawberries and the 2 tablespoons sugar. Cover and chill for at least 1 hour.

2. In another medium bowl stir together flour, the 1 tablespoon sugar, the baking powder, and baking soda. Using a pastry blender, cut in butter until the mixture resembles coarse crumbs. Combine egg and buttermilk; add to flour mixture all at once. Stir just until moistened. Drop the dough from a tablespoon into 8 mounds on an ungreased baking sheet.

3. Bake in a 450° oven for 7 to 8 minutes or until golden. Transfer the shortcakes to a wire rack; cool about 10 minutes. Meanwhile, if using topping mix, prepare according to package directions using fat-free milk.

4. To serve, cut shortcakes in half horizontally. Place bottom halves on plates. Top with strawberries and whipped topping. Replace top halves of shortcakes.

Nutrition Facts per serving: 224 cal., 8 g total fat (5 g sat. fat), 39 mg chol., 211 mg sodium, 33 g carbo., 2 g fiber, 4 g pro.
Daily Values: 5% vit. A, 51% vit. C, 9% calcium, 8% iron
Exchanges: ½ Fruit, 1½ Starch, 1½ Fat

Cheery Cherry-Peach Cobbler

Summer or winter, this homespun cobbler ends any meal on a delicious note while providing healthy helpings of fruit. The tender biscuitlike topping covers sweet golden peaches and tart red cherries.

Prep: 15 minutes   Bake: 20 minutes   Oven: 400°F   Makes: 8 servings

- 1 **cup all-purpose flour**
- 2 **tablespoons sugar**
- 1½ **teaspoons baking powder**
- ¼ **teaspoon ground nutmeg**
- 2 **tablespoons butter or margarine**
- ½ **cup sugar**
- 4 **teaspoons cornstarch**
- ⅓ **cup water**
- 3 **cups fresh or frozen unsweetened sliced, peeled peaches**
- 2 **cups fresh or frozen unsweetened pitted tart red cherries**
- ⅓ **cup plain fat-free yogurt**
- ¼ **cup refrigerated or frozen egg product, thawed**
  Frozen light whipped dessert topping, thawed (optional)

1. For topping, in a small bowl stir together the flour, the 2 tablespoons sugar, the baking powder, and the nutmeg. Using a pastry blender or 2 knives, cut in butter until mixture resembles coarse crumbs; set aside.

2. For filling, in a large saucepan stir together the ½ cup sugar and the cornstarch. Stir in the water. Add the peach slices and cherries. Cook and stir until thickened and bubbly. Keep filling hot while finishing topping.

3. Stir together the yogurt and egg product. Add yogurt mixture to topping mixture, stirring just until moistened.

4. Transfer filling to a 2-quart square baking dish. Using a spoon, immediately drop the topping from a spoon into 8 mounds onto hot filling.

5. Bake in a 400° oven about 20 minutes or until a wooden toothpick inserted into the topping comes out clean. Serve warm. If desired, top with whipped dessert topping.

Nutrition Facts per serving: 203 cal., 3 g total fat (2 g sat. fat), 8 mg chol., 128 mg sodium, 41 g carbo., 2 g fiber, 4 g pro.
Daily Values: 18% vit. A, 12% vit. C, 8% calcium, 6% iron
Exchanges: 1½ Fruit, 1 Starch, ½ Fat

150

Berry Dessert Nachos

To make this fun-to-eat, nutrient-rich dessert, layer fresh berries and fat-free whipped topping on top of cinnamon- and sugar-coated tortilla crisps. Blueberries or sliced strawberries will work too.

Prep: 20 minutes   Bake: 5 minutes   Cool: 15 minutes
Oven: 400°F   Makes: 6 servings

- ½ **cup light dairy sour cream**
- ½ **cup frozen light whipped dessert topping, thawed**
- 2 **tablespoons sugar**
- ⅛ **teaspoon ground cinnamon**
- 6 **7- to 8-inch flour tortillas**
- **Butter-flavored nonstick cooking spray**
- 1 **tablespoon sugar**
- ⅛ **teaspoon ground cinnamon**
- 3 **cups raspberries and/or blackberries**
- 2 **tablespoons sliced almonds, toasted**
- 1½ **teaspoons grated semisweet chocolate**

1. In a small bowl stir together sour cream, dessert topping, the 2 tablespoons sugar, and ⅛ teaspoon cinnamon; cover and chill.

2. Meanwhile, cut each tortilla into 8 wedges. Arrange wedges on 2 baking sheets. Lightly coat wedges with cooking spray. In a small bowl stir together the 1 tablespoon sugar and ⅛ teaspoon cinnamon; sprinkle over tortilla wedges. Bake in a 400° oven about 5 minutes or until crisp. Cool completely on a wire rack.

3. To serve, place 8 tortilla wedges on each of 6 dessert plates. Top with berries and sour cream mixture. Sprinkle with almonds and grated chocolate.

Nutrition Facts per serving: 205 cal., 7 g total fat (3 g sat. fat), 7 mg chol., 133 mg sodium, 32 g carbo., 5 g fiber, 5 g pro.
Daily Values: 4% vit. A, 26% vit. C, 9% calcium, 8% iron
Exchanges: 1 Fruit, 1 Starch, 1½ Fat

Outrageous Baked Apples

Caramel apple lovers will be fans of this dessert. It adds caramel ice cream topping to fresh apples and frozen yogurt for an awesome treat.

Prep: 25 minutes   Bake: 50 minutes   Oven: 350°F   Makes: 4 servings

2 medium cooking apples, such as Rome Beauty, Granny Smith, or Jonathan

1/4 cup raisins, dried cranberries, or mixed dried fruit bits

2 tablespoons red cinnamon candies

1 tablespoon packed brown sugar

1/3 cup apple juice or water

1/3 cup caramel ice cream topping

1 tablespoon maple-flavored syrup

1 cup vanilla frozen yogurt

Chopped walnuts or pecans, toasted (optional)

1. Core apples; peel a strip from the top of each. Place apples in a 2-quart square baking dish. Combine the raisins, cinnamon candies, and brown sugar; spoon into center of apples. Pour apple juice into baking dish. Bake, uncovered, in a 350° oven for 50 to 55 minutes or until the apples are tender, basting occasionally during baking.

2. Meanwhile, for topping, in a small bowl combine caramel topping and maple syrup; set aside.

3. To serve, halve warm apples lengthwise. Transfer apple halves to dessert dishes. Top each with a scoop of frozen yogurt. Drizzle with topping. If desired, sprinkle with nuts. Serve immediately.

Nutrition Facts per serving: 256 cal., 2 g total fat (1 g sat. fat), 5 mg chol., 81 mg sodium, 60 g carbo., 2 g fiber, 3 g pro.
Daily Values: 3% vit. A, 6% vit. C, 20% calcium, 3% iron
Exchanges: 1 1/2 Fruit, 2 1/2 Other Carbo.

Deep-Dish Apple Pie

This all-American dessert features tender apple slices spiced with cinnamon and topped with a flaky pastry crust. It's a treat the whole family will love.

Prep: 30 minutes   Bake: 40 minutes   Oven: 375°F   Makes: 8 servings

6 cups thinly sliced, peeled cooking apples (about 2 pounds total)

¼ cup sugar

1 teaspoon ground cinnamon

1 tablespoon cornstarch

⅛ teaspoon salt

¾ cup all-purpose flour or ½ cup all-purpose flour plus ¼ cup whole wheat flour

Dash ground nutmeg

3 tablespoons butter or margarine

2 to 3 tablespoons cold water

Fat-free milk

Frozen vanilla yogurt (optional)

1. Place apples in a 2-quart square baking dish.

2. In a small bowl combine sugar and cinnamon; set aside 1 teaspoon of the mixture. Stir the cornstarch and salt into the remaining sugar mixture; sprinkle evenly over the apples in the baking dish.

3. In a medium bowl stir together the flour and nutmeg. Using a pastry blender, cut in butter until pieces are pea-size. Sprinkle 1 tablespoon of the water over part of the flour mixture; gently toss with a fork. Push moistened dough to side of bowl. Repeat, using 1 tablespoon at a time, until all the flour mixture is moistened. Form into a ball.

4. On a lightly floured surface, slightly flatten dough. Roll dough from center to edges into a 10-inch square. Cut decorative vents in pastry. Carefully place pastry over apples. Using the tines of a fork, press edges to sides of dish. Brush pastry with milk and sprinkle with the reserved sugar mixture.

5. Bake in a 375° oven about 40 minutes or until the apples are tender and the crust is golden. Serve warm. If desired, serve with frozen yogurt.

Nutrition Facts per serving: 166 cal., 5 g total fat (3 g sat. fat), 12 mg chol., 84 mg sodium, 30 g carbo., 2 g fiber, 1 g pro.
Daily Values: 4% vit. A, 5% vit. C, 1% calcium, 4% iron
Exchanges: 1½ Fruit, ½ Starch, 1 Fat

Fast and Fruity Tarts

Ready in just 10 minutes, these mini tarts are the perfect sweet to close a weeknight meal. Potassium-rich bananas or other fresh fruit top the cream cheese filling.

Start to Finish: **10 minutes**   *Makes:* **15 tarts**

1 **8-ounce tub reduced-fat cream cheese**
¼ **cup strawberry, peach, pineapple, or other preserves**
1 **2.1-ounce package (15) miniature phyllo dough shells**
½ **cup cut-up banana; cut-up, peeled kiwifruit; and/or cut-up strawberries**
3 **tablespoons chocolate ice cream topping**

1. For filling, in a small bowl stir together the cream cheese and preserves. Spoon filling into each phyllo shell. If desired, cover and refrigerate for up to 4 hours.

2. To serve, divide fruit among shells. Drizzle with ice cream topping. Serve immediately.

Nutrition Facts per tart: 86 cal., 3 g total fat (2 g sat. fat), 7 mg chol., 86 mg sodium, 11 g carbo., 0 g fiber, 2 g pro.
Daily Values: 4% vit. A, 2% vit. C, 2% calcium, 1% iron
Exchanges: 1 Other Carbo., ½ Fat

Shimmering Strawberry Pie

Scrumptious, juicy strawberries pack this low-calorie version of a classic pie. Keep the oil pastry in mind when you wish to slash calories from other recipes for single-crust pies.

Prep: 1 hour   Bake: 10 minutes   Chill: 3 hours   Oven: 450°F   Makes: 8 servings

    1 recipe **Oil Pastry for Single-Crust Pie**
    6 **cups strawberries, halved**
    1 **cup water**
    ¼ **cup sugar**
    2 **tablespoons cornstarch**
      Few drops red food coloring (optional)
      Light frozen whipped dessert topping, thawed (optional)

1. Prepare Oil Pastry for Single-Crust Pie. Prick bottom and sides of pastry generously with the tines of a fork. Bake in a 450° oven for 10 to 12 minutes or until pastry is golden. Cool on a wire rack.

2. In a blender container or food processor bowl combine 1 cup of the strawberries and the water. Cover and blend or process until smooth. Transfer to a small saucepan. Bring to boiling; reduce heat. Simmer, uncovered, for 2 minutes.

3. In a medium saucepan stir together sugar and cornstarch; stir in berry mixture. Cook and stir over medium heat until thickened and bubbly. Cook and stir for 2 minutes more. Remove from heat. If desired, stir in enough red food coloring to tint a rich red color. Cool syrup mixture to room temperature.

4. Fold remaining strawberries into cooled syrup mixture; transfer mixture to pastry shell. Cover; chill for 3 to 4 hours. If desired, serve with whipped topping.

Oil Pastry for Single-Crust Pie: In a medium bowl stir together 1¼ cups all-purpose flour and ¼ teaspoon salt. Combine ¼ cup fat-free milk and 3 tablespoons cooking oil. Add milk mixture all at once to flour mixture. Stir lightly with a fork until dough forms. Form into a ball. On a lightly floured surface, slightly flatten dough. Roll dough into a 12-inch circle. Ease pastry into a 9-inch pie plate. Trim pastry to ½ inch beyond edge of plate. Fold under extra pastry; crimp edge as desired.

Nutrition Facts per serving: 182 cal., 6 g total fat (1 g sat. fat), 0 mg chol., 79 mg sodium, 31 g carbo., 3 g fiber, 3 g pro.
Daily Values: 1% vit. A, 103% vit. C, 3% calcium, 8% iron
Exchanges: 1 Fruit, 1 Starch, 1 Fat

Mini Mint Mouthfuls

Your turn to bring treats? Make these candy-topped chocolate cookies—children are sure to love them.

Prep: *20 minutes* Chill: *1 hour* Bake: *8 minutes per batch*
Oven: *350°F* Makes: *about 48 cookies*

  1 **cup all-purpose flour**
  ¼ **teaspoon baking soda**
  ¼ **cup butter or margarine**
  ⅔ **cup granulated sugar**
  ⅓ **cup unsweetened cocoa powder**
  ¼ **cup packed brown sugar**
  ¼ **cup buttermilk**
  1 **teaspoon vanilla**
    Nonstick cooking spray
  ¼ **cup granulated sugar**
  48 **miniature chocolate-covered cream-filled mint patties (⅔ cup)**

1. In a small bowl stir together flour and baking soda; set aside.

2. In a medium saucepan melt butter; remove from heat. Stir in the ⅔ cup granulated sugar, the cocoa power, and brown sugar. Stir in buttermilk and vanilla. Stir in flour mixture just until combined. Chill dough for 1 hour. (Dough will be stiff.)

3. Lightly coat cookie sheets with cooking spray; set aside. Shape dough into 1-inch balls. Roll balls in the ¼ cup granulated sugar. Place 2 inches apart on prepared cookie sheets.

4. Bake in a 350° oven for 8 to 10 minutes or until edges are firm. Immediately, press a mint pattie into the center of each cookie. Cool on cookie sheet for 1 minute. Transfer to a wire rack and let cool.

Nutrition Facts per cookie: 50 cal., 1 g total fat (1 g sat. fat), 3 mg chol.,
23 mg sodium, 9 g carbo., 0 g fiber, 0 g pro.
Daily Values: 1% vit. A, 1% calcium, 2% iron
Exchanges: ½ Other Carbo.

Lunch Box Oatmeal Cookies

This recipe combines two kid favorites—oatmeal and peanut butter—into one great tasting cookie. Using reduced-fat peanut butter and egg whites in place of whole eggs keeps the fat content low.

Prep: *25 minutes*   Bake: *7 minutes per batch*
Oven: *375°F*   Makes: *about 40 cookies*

½ **cup butter or margarine, softened**
½ **cup reduced-fat peanut butter**
⅓ **cup granulated sugar**
⅓ **cup packed brown sugar**
½ **teaspoon baking soda**
2 **egg whites**
½ **teaspoon vanilla**
1 **cup all-purpose flour**
1 **cup quick-cooking rolled oats**

1. In a large mixing bowl beat butter and peanut butter with an electric mixer on medium to high speed about 30 seconds or until combined.

2. Add granulated sugar, brown sugar, and baking soda. Beat until combined, scraping sides of bowl occasionally. Beat in egg whites and vanilla until combined. Beat in as much flour as you can with the mixer. Stir in any remaining flour. Stir in oats.

3. Drop dough by rounded teaspoons 2 inches apart on ungreased cookie sheets. Bake in a 375° oven for 7 to 8 minutes or until edges are golden. Cool on cookie sheet for 1 minute. Transfer to a wire rack and let cool.

Nutrition Facts per cookie:
76 cal., 4 g total fat (2 g sat. fat), 7 mg chol., 69 mg sodium, 9 g carbo., 1 g fiber, 2 g pro.
Daily Values: 2% vit. A, 1% calcium, 2% iron
Exchanges: ½ Other Carbo., ½ Fat

Luscious Lemon Triangles

Perfectly sweet and refreshingly tart describe these impressive cookie bars.

Prep: 25 minutes *Bake:* 35 minutes *Cool:* 1 hour
Oven: 350°F *Makes:* 18 triangles

Nonstick cooking spray
¾ cup all-purpose flour
3 tablespoons granulated sugar
¼ cup butter or margarine
1 egg
1 egg white
⅔ cup granulated sugar
2 tablespoons all-purpose flour
1 teaspoon finely shredded lemon peel (set aside)
2 tablespoons lemon juice
1 tablespoon water
¼ teaspoon baking powder
Sifted powdered sugar (optional)

1. Lightly coat an 8×8×2-inch baking pan with cooking spray; set aside. In a small bowl combine the ¾ cup flour and the 3 tablespoons granulated sugar. Using a pastry blender or 2 knives, cut in butter until mixture resembles coarse crumbs. Press mixture into the bottom of the prepared pan. Bake in a 350° oven for 15 minutes.

2. Meanwhile, for filling, in a small mixing bowl combine the egg and egg white. Beat with an electric mixer on medium speed until frothy. Add the ⅔ cup granulated sugar, the 2 tablespoons flour, the lemon juice, water, and baking powder. Beat on medium speed for 3 minutes or until slightly thickened. Stir in lemon peel. Pour filling over hot crust.

3. Bake for 20 to 25 minutes more or until edges are light brown and center is set. Cool on a wire rack. Cut into 9 squares; cut each square diagonally to make a triangle. If desired, sprinkle with sifted powdered sugar.

Nutrition Facts per triangle: 85 cal., 3 g total fat (2 g sat. fat), 19 mg chol., 40 mg sodium, 14 g carbo., 0 g fiber, 1 g pro.
Daily Values: 2% vit. A, 2% vit. C, 1% calcium, 2% iron
Exchanges: 1 Other Carbo., ½ Fat

Pineapple-Topped Ice Cream

Applaud a good report card or soccer victory with these hot pineapple-and-orange sundaes. They're festive enough for noteworthy occasions and encourage your child to eat more fruit.

Start to Finish: 12 minutes   Makes: 6 servings

- ½ **teaspoon finely shredded orange peel**
- ¼ **cup orange juice**
- 2 **teaspoons cornstarch**
- ½ **teaspoon ground ginger**
- 1 **20-ounce can crushed pineapple (juice pack), undrained**
- 1½ **cups vanilla low-fat or light ice cream or frozen yogurt**

1. In a large skillet stir together orange peel, juice, cornstarch, and ground ginger. Stir in undrained pineapple. Cook and stir over medium heat until slightly thickened and bubbly. Cook and stir for 2 minutes more. Remove from heat. Serve immediately over ice cream.

Nutrition Facts per serving: 120 cal., 1 g total fat (1 g sat. fat), 3 mg chol., 26 mg sodium, 27 g carbo., 1 g fiber, 1 g pro.
Daily Values: 3% vit. A, 24% vit. C, 6% calcium, 2% iron
Exchanges: 1 Fruit, 1 Other Carbo.

Fun Day Sundae Parfait

Summer fun never ends when you serve these showstopping parfaits. This layered frozen yogurt dessert entices finicky eaters.

Start to Finish: 15 minutes   *Makes: 2 servings*

1½ **cups frozen vanilla or fruit-flavored yogurt or light ice cream**

½ **cup coarsely crushed vanilla wafers or honey or cinnamon graham crackers**

1 **cup fresh fruit, such as sliced bananas or strawberries; peeled, sliced kiwifruit, peaches, or mangoes; cut-up pineapple; raspberries; and/or blueberries**

6 **tablespoons strawberry ice cream topping**

¼ **cup frozen light whipped dessert topping, thawed (optional)**

2 **maraschino cherries with stems (optional)**

1. Chill 2 tall parfait glasses.

2. Place ¼ cup frozen yogurt in the bottom of each chilled glass. Top each with 2 tablespoons of the crushed wafers, ¼ cup fruit, and 1 tablespoon strawberry topping. Repeat layers. Top each with ¼ cup frozen yogurt. Drizzle each with remaining strawberry topping. If desired, top with whipped topping and garnish with maraschino cherries. Serve with long-handled spoons.

162

Nutrition Facts per serving: 375 cal., 9 g total fat (4 g sat. fat), 15 mg chol., 138 mg sodium, 70 g carbo., 2 g fiber, 4 g pro.
Daily Values: 6% vit. A, 68% vit. C, 46% calcium, 3% iron
Exchanges: 1 Fruit, 3½ Other Carbo., 1½ Fat

My Mom's Chocolate Pudding

Try this old-fashioned chocolate pudding with improved nutritional value: It's loaded with creamy chocolate goodness and low in calories, fat, and cholesterol.

Prep: 20 minutes   Chill: 4 to 24 hours   Makes: 6 servings

- 1/3 **cup sugar**
- 3 **tablespoons all-purpose flour**
- 3 **tablespoons unsweetened cocoa powder**
- 2 1/4 **cups fat-free milk**
- 2 **teaspoons butter or margarine**
- 1 1/2 **teaspoons vanilla**
- 1 **medium banana, sliced, or** 1/2 **cup fresh blueberries, raspberries, or sliced strawberries (optional)**

1. In a heavy medium saucepan stir together the sugar, flour, and cocoa powder. Stir in milk. Cook and stir over medium heat until thickened and bubbly. Cook and stir for 1 minute more. Remove from the heat. Stir in the butter and vanilla.

2. Spoon the pudding into 6 dessert dishes. Cover surface of pudding with plastic wrap. Chill for 4 to 24 hours. If desired, serve with fresh fruit.

164

Nutrition Facts per serving: 113 cal., 2 g total fat (1 g sat. fat), 5 mg chol., 62 mg sodium, 19 g carbo., 0 g fiber, 4 g pro.
Daily Values: 5% vit. A, 2% vit. C, 14% calcium, 3% iron
Exchanges: 1/2 Milk, 1 Other Carbo.

What's life without a little dessert?

If you're concerned about how much sugar or empty calories your child is eating, don't ban dessert from your table. When sweets are forbidden your kids may crave them that much more! If you want to feel better about ending a meal on a sweet note, serve a fruit-based dessert, make your cookies miniature size, serve sorbet instead of ice cream, and portion each serving so there are no sneaky seconds.

Georgie Porgie Pudding

Who can resist the combination of chocolate and peanut butter?
Stir these two well-loved flavors into one astounding pudding.

Prep: 10 minutes Chill: 1 hour Makes: 4 servings

1 **4-serving-size package instant chocolate-flavored pudding mix**

1¾ **cups cold milk**

1 **tablespoon reduced-fat peanut butter**

1 **tablespoon chopped honey-roasted peanuts**

¼ **of an 8-ounce container frozen light whipped dessert topping, thawed**

2 **tablespoons chopped peanuts**

Graham snack cookies (optional)

1. In a large mixing bowl beat pudding mix, cold milk, and peanut butter with a wire whisk for 2 minutes. Stir in peanuts. Divide pudding evenly among 4 dessert dishes.

2. Cover surface of pudding with plastic wrap. Chill for 1 to 2 hours. Just before serving, top each with a dollop of dessert topping and sprinkle with peanuts. If desired, serve with graham snack cookies.

Nutrition Facts per serving: 245 cal., 8 g total fat (4 g sat. fat), 9 mg chol., 522 mg sodium, 36 g carbo., 1 g fiber, 6 g pro.
Daily Values: 5% vit. A, 2% vit. C, 14% calcium, 3% iron
Exchanges: ½ Milk, 2 Other Carbo., 1½ Fat

IT'S PARTY TIME

Kids love a party whether they're celebrating a birthday, the last day of school, or a favorite holiday. With the festive, good-for-you recipes on the following pages, you can treat your children and their friends to an afternoon of fun and nutritious food. Instead of sugary cakes and packaged chips, plan a party around these easy-to-make, vitamin-packed sandwiches, snacks, and sweets. Pretty soon, the other parents will be asking you for the recipes.

8

Fizzy Fruit Slush, Queso Dip with
Tortilla Stars, and Birthday Brownie
and Ice Cream Cake

HAPPY BIRTHDAY BASH

Have your cake—and ice cream too! This trio of kids' favorites will make your next birthday bash a smash! And because mom should enjoy the party too, make the punch and brownie the day before.

Fizzy Fruit Slush

A triple dose of fruit—pineapple juice, peach slices, and melon cubes—blends into a colorful slush that gets pizzazz from sparkling water.

Start to Finish: **20 minutes**   *Makes:* **12 (about 6-ounce) servings**

- **I 12-ounce can frozen pineapple juice concentrate, thawed**
- **I 15-ounce can peach slices (juice pack), chilled and drained**
- **4 cups cubed, seeded watermelon or sliced fresh strawberries**
- **I I-liter bottle sparkling water with strawberry or peach flavor**
- **Crushed ice**

1. In a blender container or food processor bowl combine pineapple juice concentrate, drained peaches, and watermelon or strawberries. Cover and blend or process until smooth. If desired, strain the strawberry mixture through a fine-mesh sieve to remove seeds. Transfer fruit mixture to a large pitcher. Chill, if desired.

2. To serve, slowly stir sparkling water into fruit mixture. Serve immediately over crushed ice.

Nutrition Facts per serving: 98 cal., 0 g total fat (0 g sat. fat), 0 mg chol., 11 mg sodium, 24 g carbo., 1 g fiber, 1 g pro.
Daily Values: 7% vit. A, 35% vit. C, 2% calcium, 3% iron
Exchanges: 1 Fruit, 1/2 Other Carbo.

168

Queso Dip with Tortilla Stars

Have plenty of napkins on hand. This dip is so good, kids will try to load lots of it on their chips or vegetables. The star-shaped dippers are festive, but if you're short on time, cut the tortillas into wedges.

Start to Finish: **30 minutes** *Oven:* **350°F** *Makes:* **2¼ cups (2 tablespoons per serving)**

- ¼ **cup chopped onion**
- 2 **cloves garlic, minced**
- 2 **tablespoons water**
- 1 **14½-ounce can stewed tomatoes, drained and cut up**
- 1 **4½-ounce can chopped green chile peppers, drained**
- ½ **to ¾ teaspoon chili powder**
- ¼ **teaspoon bottled hot pepper sauce**
- 1 **cup shredded reduced-fat cheddar cheese (4 ounces)**
- 3 **ounces cream cheese, cubed**
- 3 **ounces fat-free cream cheese, cubed**
- 1 **recipe Tortilla Stars and/or cut-up fresh vegetables**

1. In a 2-quart saucepan combine onion, garlic, and water. Bring to boiling. Cook, uncovered, over medium heat for 2 to 3 minutes or until water has evaporated. Add tomatoes, chiles, chili powder, and hot pepper sauce. Cook and stir until heated through. Add cheddar cheese and cream cheeses. Cook and stir over low heat until cheese is melted. Serve immediately with Tortilla Stars and/or fresh vegetables.

169

Tortilla Stars: Using a star-shaped cookie cutter, cut stars from nine 7- or 8-inch flour tortillas. (Or cut each tortilla into 8 wedges). Spread one-third of the stars in a 15×10×1-inch baking pan. If desired, place stars over bunched foil in baking pan. Bake in a 350° oven for 5 to 10 minutes or until dry and crisp. Repeat with remaining stars; cool. Store in an airtight container at room temperature up to 4 days or in the freezer up to 3 weeks. Makes 72 (18 appetizer servings).

Nutrition Facts per 2 tablespoons dip: 96 cal., 4 g total fat (2 g sat. fat), 10 mg chol., 231 mg sodium, 10 g carbo., 1 g fiber, 4 g pro.
Daily Values: 7% vit. A, 7% vit. C, 8% calcium, 4% iron
Exchanges: ½ Starch, 1 Fat

Birthday Brownie and Ice Cream Cake

This oversize ice cream-filled brownie will be the hit of your child's next birthday party. It's ice cream and cake all rolled into one.

Prep: 25 minutes   Bake: 20 minutes   Stand: 10 minutes   Freeze: at least 3 hours
Oven: 350°F   Makes: 12 servings

- 1 **20.5-ounce package low-fat brownie mix**
- 4 **cups (1 quart) vanilla, chocolate, or chocolate chip-flavored low fat or light ice cream, softened**
- ¾ **cup chocolate-flavored syrup**

1. Line the bottoms of two 9×1½-inch round baking pans with waxed paper. Grease waxed paper or coat with nonstick cooking spray; set aside.

2. Prepare brownie mix according to package directions. Divide batter evenly between prepared pans, spreading batter to edges of pans.

3. Bake in a 350° oven for 20 minutes. Cool in pans on wire racks for 10 minutes. Remove layers from pans; peel off waxed paper. Cool completely.

4. To assemble, place one brownie on a serving plate, top side down. Spread softened ice cream over brownie. Place second brownie, top side up, on the ice cream. Freeze for at least 3 hours or until firm. (Cover with foil for longer storage.)

5. To serve, let stand at room temperature 10 minutes. Using a large, sharp knife, cut into 12 wedges. Place on individual serving plates. Drizzle each with chocolate-flavored syrup. Serve immediately.

Nutrition Facts per serving: 320 cal., 5 g total fat (2 g sat. fat), 3 mg chol., 220 mg sodium, 67 g carbo., 2 g fiber, 5 g pro.
Daily Values: 3% vit. A, 7% calcium, 10% iron
Exchanges: 4½ Other Carbo., 1 Fat

VALENTINE'S DAY DELIGHTS

Who can say no to pizza, a swirly fruit dip, and sweet cherry tarts? From grade school kiddos to the teenagers in your house, everyone will love these festive flavors.

Be Mine Pizza

Declare undying affection on Valentine's Day by sharing this pizza with your loved ones.

Prep: 20 minutes *Bake:* 12 minutes
Cool: 5 minutes *Oven:* 400°F
Makes: 6 servings (2 each)

Nonstick cooking spray
12 thin slices mozzarella cheese (12 ounces)
1 10-ounce package refrigerated pizza dough
1 8-ounce can pizza sauce
½ cup sliced turkey pepperoni or Canadian-style bacon (2 ounces)
2 tablespoons grated Parmesan cheese

1. Lightly coat a large baking sheet with cooking spray; set aside. Using a 2½- to 3-inch heart-shaped cutter, cut heart shapes from cheese slices. Set cutouts aside. (Save scraps for another use.)

2. Unroll pizza dough onto the prepared baking sheet. Roll to a 16×12-inch rectangle. Spread pizza sauce over pizza dough. Arrange pepperoni over sauce. Sprinkle with Parmesan cheese.

3. Bake in a 400° oven for 10 minutes. Add cheese cutouts and bake 2 to 3 minutes more or until cheese melts and crust is golden. Cool on a wire rack 5 minutes. Cut into 12 squares.

Nutrition Facts per serving: 239 cal., 8 g total fat (4 g sat. fat), 30 mg chol., 611 mg sodium, 25 g carbo., 1 g dietary fiber, 15 g protein.
Daily Values: 11% vit. A, 6% vit. C, 21% calcium, 10% iron.
Exchanges: 1 vegetable, 1 starch, 1 lean meat, 1 fat

Lovin' Lemon Swirl Dip

A little lemon adds zing to this creamy fruit dip. Serve it on a tray surrounded by mounds of fresh fruit. Photo, page 171.

Prep: 10 minutes   Chill: 1 to 24 hours   Makes: 6 servings

- 1 **8-ounce container vanilla low-fat yogurt**
- ¼ **teaspoon finely shredded lemon peel**
- 1 **tablespoon lemon juice**
- **Dash ground cinnamon**
- **Dash ground ginger**
- 3 **tablespoons strawberry jam or preserves**
- 3 **cups assorted fresh fruit such as apple and/or pear wedges*, plum slices, strawberries, raspberries, and/or seedless grapes**

1. In a medium bowl stir together yogurt, lemon peel, lemon juice, cinnamon, and ginger. Cover and chill for 1 to 24 hours.

2. To serve, transfer yogurt mixture to individual serving dishes or a serving bowl. Drop small spoonfuls of jam over yogurt mixture. Using a thin knife, gently swirl jam into yogurt mixture. Arrange fresh fruit on a serving platter. Serve fruit with swirled yogurt mixture.

*Note: To prevent apples and pears from turning brown, place the sliced fruit in a bowl. Add 2 tablespoons lemon juice and 2 tablespoons water; toss to coat. Drain. If desired, pat dry with paper towels.

Nutrition Facts per serving: 100 cal., 1 g total fat (0 g sat. fat), 2 mg chol., 28 mg sodium, 22 g carbo., 2 g fiber, 2 g pro.
Daily Values: 3% vit. A, 12% vit. C, 7% calcium, 1% iron
Exchanges: 1 Fruit, ½ Other Carbo.

Cherry-Berry Sweetie Pies

Mini ginger-spiced tarts filled with red cherries and berries make the perfect gift for your sweeties on Valentine's Day. Photo, page 171.

Prep: 40 minutes   Bake: 25 minutes   Cool: 1 hour   Oven: 325°F   Makes: 24 tarts

1 cup all-purpose flour
1/4 cup packed brown sugar
1/4 teaspoon ground cinnamon
1/8 teaspoon ground ginger
1/3 cup butter or margarine
2 to 3 tablespoons cold water
1/4 cup granulated sugar
1 tablespoon cornstarch
1/4 cup water
3/4 cup frozen pitted tart cherries
1/2 cup frozen raspberries or blueberries
1 recipe **Vanilla Drizzle**

1. For pastry, in a medium bowl stir together flour, brown sugar, cinnamon, and ginger. Using a pastry blender, cut in butter until mixture resembles coarse crumbs. Gradually add the 2 to 3 tablespoons water, tossing gently with a fork until dough forms. Press a rounded teaspoon of the dough evenly into the bottom and up the sides of 24 ungreased 1 3/4-inch muffin cups.

2. For filling, in a small saucepan stir together granulated sugar and cornstarch; stir in the 1/4 cup water. Add frozen cherries and berries. Cook and stir over medium heat until thickened and bubbly. Remove saucepan from heat. Spoon 1 rounded teaspoon of filling into each pastry-lined muffin cup.

3. Bake in a 325° oven for 25 to 30 minutes or until crust is golden. Cool slightly in pan. Carefully transfer to a wire rack and let cool. To serve, drizzle each tart with Vanilla Drizzle.

Vanilla Drizzle: In a small bowl combine 1/2 cup sifted powdered sugar, 1/2 teaspoon vanilla, and enough milk (2 to 3 teaspoons) to make icing drizzling consistency.

Presentation Idea: For a Valentine's Day party, arrange tarts in a large heart shape on a large serving platter.

Nutrition Facts per tart: 73 cal., 3 g total fat (2 g sat. fat), 7 mg chol., 29 mg sodium, 12 g carbo., 0 g fiber, 1 g pro.
Daily Values: 3% vit. A, 1% calcium, 2% iron
Exchanges: 1 Fruit, 1/2 Fat

LET'S GO SLEDDING

Brrr! A warm mug of cider and a slice of snowy angel food cake really hit the spot after some winter weather outdoor fun.

Sugar 'n' Spice Cider

Warm cold hands with a cup of this hot and spicy cider. Kids love stirring it with sugarcoated cinnamon sticks.

Prep: 15 minutes   *Cook:* 15 minutes   *Stand:* 30 minutes
Makes: 8 (about 8-ounce) servings

174

- 8 **cups apple cider or apple juice**
- 2 **tablespoons honey**
- 6 **inches stick cinnamon**
- 2 **teaspoons chopped crystallized ginger**
- 1 **teaspoon whole cloves**
- 1 **recipe Sugared Cinnamon Sticks**

1. In a large saucepan combine cider and honey. For spice bag, place stick cinnamon, crystallized ginger, and cloves in center of a double-thick, 6-inch square of 100-percent-cotton cheesecloth. Bring corners of the cheesecloth together and tie with a clean string. Add spice bag to the saucepan with cider mixture.

2. Bring mixture to boiling; reduce heat. Simmer, covered, for 10 minutes. Remove spice bag and discard. Serve cider in mugs. Garnish with Sugared Cinnamon Sticks.

Sugared Cinnamon Sticks: Place 3 tablespoons coarse sugar in a shallow dish. For each stick, lightly brush half of a 3- to 4-inch cinnamon stick with light-colored corn syrup. Roll in sugar. Place on waxed paper. Let stand at room temperature about 30 minutes or until dry.

Nutrition Facts per serving: 156 cal., 0 g total fat (0 g sat. fat), 0 mg chol., 22 mg sodium, 35 g carbo., 0 g fiber, 0 g pro.
Daily Values: 4% vit. C, 2% calcium, 4% iron
Exchanges: 2 Fruit, ½ Other Carbo.

Snow Angel Cake

This all-white dessert—angel food cake topped with whipped dessert topping, white chocolate, and coconut—provides an energy boost after a long day of sledding.

Start to Finish: 15 minutes   *Makes:* 12 servings

1 purchased angel food cake
2 ounces white chocolate baking squares or 1/3 cup vanilla milk pieces
1 8-ounce container frozen light whipped dessert topping, thawed
1/4 cup coconut

1. Place cake on a serving plate; set aside.

2. In a small saucepan melt white chocolate over low heat, stirring occasionally. Remove from heat.

3. Frost cake with whipped topping. Sprinkle with coconut. Drizzle with melted white chocolate.

Nutrition Facts per serving: 154 cal., 5 g total fat (4 g sat. fat), 1 mg chol., 225 mg sodium, 24 g carbo., 1 g fiber, 2 g pro.
Daily Values: 5% calcium, 1% iron
Exchanges: 1 1/2 Other Carbo., 1 Fat

GHOULISH GATHERING

Host the witches, ghosts, and goblins you love the most for a Halloween treat. Instead of bobbing for apples, dive into Caramel Apple Sundaes and nibble on Monster Morsels. Delight in a little sip of Ghoul's Punch—just watch out for floating fingers!

Bewitching Caramel Apple Sundaes

Perfect for Halloween—these healthful sundaes use chopped red and green apples instead of ice cream. They are a great way to add fiber and vitamins to kids' diets.

Start to Finish: 25 minutes   Makes: 8 servings

   2 medium red apples, cored and coarsely chopped
   2 medium green apples, cored and coarsely chopped
   1 tablespoon lemon juice
   ½ cup caramel ice cream topping
   ½ of an 8-ounce container frozen light whipped dessert topping, thawed
   1 cup low-fat granola or toasted corn and wheat cereal flakes with oats

1. In a large bowl toss together red apples, green apples, and lemon juice.

2. Divide the apple mixture among 8 dessert dishes. Drizzle each with 1 tablespoon ice cream topping. Spoon whipped dessert topping on each. Sprinkle each with 2 tablespoons of the cereal. Serve immediately.

Nutrition Facts per serving: 180 cal., 3 g total fat (2 g sat. fat), 0 mg chol., 75 mg sodium, 38 g carbo., 3 g fiber, 2 g pro.
Daily Values: 4% vit. A, 9% vit. C, 4% calcium, 3% iron
Exchanges: 1 Fruit, ½ Starch, 1 Other Carbo., ½ Fat

Monster Morsels

Three ingredients and 20 minutes are all it takes to bake these sweet, bite-size rolls—a favorite treat of little ghosts and goblins.

Prep: 10 minutes   Bake: 10 minutes   Oven: 350°F   Makes: 12 servings (48 pieces)

- ¼ **cup sugar or orange-colored sugar**
- ½ **teaspoon pumpkin pie spice**
- 1 **11.5-ounce package (8) refrigerated breadsticks**

1. In a shallow dish stir together sugar and pumpkin pie spice. Unroll breadsticks. Separate and cut into 1-inch pieces. Roll each piece in the sugar mixture, coating pieces on all sides. Place on an ungreased baking sheet.

2. Bake in a 350° oven about 10 minutes or until bottoms are light brown. Serve warm.

Nutrition Facts per serving:
92 cal., 2 g total fat (0 g sat. fat),
0 mg chol., 202 mg sodium,
17 g carbo., 0 g fiber, 2 g pro.
Daily Values: 4% iron
Exchanges: 1 Starch

Ghoul's Punch

Frozen cranberry juice "hands" and blood-red orange slices add a ghostly touch to this pineapple-lemonade punch. What a nutritious way to serve up Halloween fun!

Prep: 20 minutes   Freeze: 8 to 24 hours   Makes: 8 (about 10-ounce) servings

> **6 cups unsweetened pineapple juice, chilled**
>
> **3 cups cold water**
>
> **1 6-ounce can frozen lemonade concentrate**
>
> **4 blood orange or orange slices**
>
> **1 recipe Frozen Hands**

1. For punch, in a punch bowl stir together pineapple juice, water, and lemonade concentrate. Float orange slices and Frozen Hands in punch.

Frozen Hands: Carefully pour cranberry juice cocktail into 2 or 3 clear plastic gloves.* Fill the gloves so that the fingers can move easily. Tightly seal the gloves with rubber bands. Place on a baking sheet lined with paper towels. Freeze until firm. Use scissors to cut the gloves off the frozen hands. If any fingers break off, add them separately to punch.

*Note: Be sure to use gloves without powder. Or rinse powdered gloves thoroughly before using.

178

Nutrition Facts per serving:
208 cal., 0 g total fat (0 g sat. fat),
0 mg chol., 8 mg sodium,
52 g carbo., 0 g fiber, 1 g pro.
Daily Values: 1% vit. A,
139% vit. C, 4% calcium, 5% iron
Exchanges: 2 Fruit,
1½ Other Carbo.

SCHOOL'S OUT

Another year of hard work is over! Welcome the lazy days of summer with this chilly, no-one-has-to-cook menu. It's a threesome of kid favorites that really makes the grade.

Turkey Taco Sandwiches

Shredded cheddar cheese and taco seasoning turn everyday turkey salad sandwiches into party-perfect food. Photo, page 181.

Prep: 15 minutes   Chill: 1 to 4 hours   Makes: 8 servings

- 3 cups chopped cooked turkey or chicken
- ½ cup shredded reduced-fat cheddar cheese (2 ounces)
- ½ cup light mayonnaise dressing or salad dressing
- 1 tablespoon milk
- 2 teaspoons taco seasoning mix
- 8 hamburger buns, split
- 1 cup shredded lettuce
- ⅓ cup finely chopped tomato (1 small)

1. In a medium bowl combine turkey and cheese. For dressing, in a small bowl stir together mayonnaise dressing, milk, and taco seasoning. Pour over turkey mixture; toss lightly to coat. Cover and chill for 1 to 4 hours.

2. To serve, spoon about ⅓ cup turkey mixture on bottoms of buns. Top with lettuce and tomato. Add bun tops. Serve immediately.

Nutrition Facts per serving: 265 cal., 7 g total fat (3 g sat. fat), 48 mg chol., 536 mg sodium, 27 g carbo., 2 g fiber, 21 g pro.
Daily Values: 4% vit. A, 4% vit. C, 14% calcium, 14% iron
Exchanges: 2 Starch, 2 Lean Meat

ABC Sandwich Cookies

Celebrate the last day of school by munching down the alphabet. Alphabet cookies filled with strawberry preserves and cream cheese disappear almost as fast as schoolbooks.

Start to Finish: 15 minutes   *Makes:* 16 cookie sandwiches

- 2 ounces reduced-fat cream cheese (tub-style)
- 1 tablespoon strawberry preserves
- Red food coloring (optional)
- 32 alphabet low-fat plain and/or chocolate shortbread cookies

1. In a small bowl stir together the cream cheese and strawberry preserves. If desired, stir in a drop of red food coloring. Spread cream cheese mixture on the flat side of half of the cookies. Top with the remaining cookies, flat side down.

Nutrition Facts per cookie sandwich: 36 cal., 1 g total fat (1 g sat. fat), 2 mg chol., 38 mg sodium, 6 g carbo., 0 g fiber, 1 g pro.
Daily Values: 1% vit. A, 1% iron
Exchanges: ½ Other Carbo.

Summertime Fruit Salad

Fruit-flavored, custard-style yogurt heightens the flavors of summer-fresh fruits in this rejuvenating hot weather salad.

Start to Finish: 25 minutes   *Makes:* 8 servings

- 2 cups sliced fresh nectarines or peaches (peeled, if desired)
- 2 cups fresh blueberries
- 2 cups sliced fresh strawberries
- 2 6-ounce containers strawberry, raspberry, or lemon low-fat custard-style yogurt
- ½ cup graham snack cookies or coarsely crushed vanilla wafers

1. In 8 clear serving dishes or a clear 2-quart bowl layer nectarines, blueberries, and strawberries. Spread yogurt over fruit. Top with graham snack cookies. Serve immediately.

Nutrition Facts per serving: 111 cal., 2 g total fat (1 g sat. fat), 4 mg chol., 43 mg sodium, 22 g carbo., 2 g fiber, 3 g pro.
Daily Values: 6% vit. A, 45% vit. C, 6% calcium, 2% iron
Exchanges: 1 Fruit, ½ Other Carbo.

SUMMER SPLASH

Invite the neighborhood gang over for some fun in the sun at the pool. No cooking required, this refreshing menu is so simple. Toss together the salad and make the punch the day before. Assemble the sandwiches that morning.

Sparkling Starfish Punch

White cranberry juice and lemonade blend into a refreshing punch sure to quench the thirst of any kid on the block.

Prep: 15 minutes   Freeze: 3 hours   Makes: 8 (about 12-ounce) servings

- 16 **thin slices star fruit (carambola), seeded**
  Lime peel strips (optional)
- 2 **cups white cranberry juice or white grape juice, chilled**
- 1 **12-ounce can frozen lemonade concentrate, thawed**
- 1 **1-liter bottle club soda, chilled**

1. Place 1 slice of star fruit in each compartment of an ice cube tray. If necessary, cut slices in half or allow points to protrude from top. If desired, add 1 or 2 lime peel strips to each compartment. Fill with water. Freeze about 3 hours or until solid.

2. Pour cranberry juice and lemonade concentrate into a 2-quart pitcher. Stir until mixed.

3. Slowly pour the club soda into the juice mixture. Put 2 of the ice cubes in each of 8 glasses. Pour lemonade mixture into each glass.

Nutrition Facts per serving: 114 cal., 0 g total fat (0 g sat. fat), 0 mg chol., 37 mg sodium, 29 g carbo., 1 g fiber, 0 g pro.
Daily Values: 3% vit. A, 53% vit. C, 1% calcium, 2% iron
Exchanges: 1 Fruit, 1 Other Carbo.

Deli-Style Submarines

Playing in water burns lots of energy. Refuel hungry tummies with thick slices of this hearty meat and cheese sandwich.

Start to Finish: 20 minutes   Makes: 8 servings

- 1 16-ounce loaf French bread
- ½ of an 8-ounce container light dairy sour cream ranch dip
- ¾ cup shredded carrot (1 large)
- 1 cup shredded lettuce
- ¾ cup shredded, seeded cucumber (½ of a medium)
- 8 ounces thinly sliced assorted deli meats (such as roast beef, ham, or turkey)
- 4 ounces thinly sliced mozzarella or provolone cheese

1. Slice French bread in half lengthwise. Spread cut sides of bread with dip. Layer carrot, lettuce, cucumber, meat, and cheese on bottom of bread. Top with top portion of bread. Cut into 8 pieces. Secure with decorative toothpicks.

Make-Ahead Directions: Wrap sandwich in plastic wrap and chill for up to 4 hours. Slice and serve as directed above.

Nutrition Facts per serving:
250 cal., 6 g total fat (3 g sat. fat), 24 mg chol., 743 mg sodium, 34 g carbo., 2 g fiber, 14 g pro.
Daily Values: 71% vit. A, 5% vit. C, 17% calcium, 9% iron
Exchanges: ½ Vegetable, 2 Starch, 1½ Lean Meat

Seashell Salad

Chilled, crisp vegetables mingle with shell pasta and crunchy sunflower seeds in creamy mustard dressing, making this an ideal salad for hot summer days. Photo, page 183.

Prep: *25 minutes*   Chill: *4 to 24 hours*   Makes: *8 servings*

8 ounces dried small shell macaroni (about 3 cups)
1 cup thinly sliced celery (2 stalks)
½ cup chopped yellow sweet pepper (1 small)
2 tablespoons thinly sliced green onion (1)
⅔ cup light dairy sour cream
⅓ cup milk
¼ cup grated Parmesan cheese
1 tablespoon Dijon-style mustard
¼ teaspoon salt
⅛ teaspoon black pepper
Milk (optional)
¼ cup shelled sunflower seeds

1. Cook macaroni according to package directions; drain. Rinse with cold water; drain again.

2. In a large bowl combine cooked macaroni, celery, sweet pepper, and green onion; set aside.

3. For dressing, in a small bowl stir together sour cream, the ⅓ cup milk, the Parmesan cheese, mustard, salt, and black pepper. Pour dressing over macaroni mixture; toss lightly to coat. Cover and chill for 4 to 24 hours. Before serving, if necessary, stir in additional milk to moisten. Stir in sunflower seeds.

Nutrition Facts per serving: 182 cal., 5 g total fat (2 g sat. fat),
9 mg chol., 187 mg sodium, 25 g carbo., 2 g fiber, 8 g pro.
Daily Values: 5% vit. A, 55% vit. C, 10% calcium, 7% iron
Exchanges: ½ Vegetable, 1½ Starch, 1 Fat

GAME DAY CELEBRATION

After the big game, invite the team to your house for dinner. You can't lose with this hearty pasta dish, garlic rolls, and a big scoop of frozen fun for dessert.

Coach's Favorite Spaghetti Sauce

Pepperoni, onion, and sweet pepper liven up everyday spaghetti sauce making this the perfect entrée after a hard-played game. Photo, page 187.

Start to Finish: **30 minutes**   *Makes:* **8 servings**

½ **cup finely chopped onion (1 medium)**
½ **cup chopped red sweet pepper (1 small)**
1 **clove garlic, minced**
1 **tablespoon olive oil**
1 **25- to 26-ounce jar tomato pasta sauce**
1 **8-ounce can low-sodium tomato sauce**
2 **ounces turkey pepperoni, halved**
1 **2¼-ounce can sliced pitted ripe olives, drained (optional)**
Hot cooked gemelli, rotini, or other pasta

1. For sauce, in a large saucepan cook onion, pepper, and garlic in hot oil over medium heat until tender, stirring occasionally. Add pasta sauce, tomato sauce, and pepperoni. Bring to boiling; reduce heat. Simmer, covered, for 10 minutes, stirring occasionally. If desired, stir in olives.

2. Serve sauce over hot cooked pasta.

Nutrition Facts per serving: 341 cal., 7 g total fat (2 g sat. fat), 9 mg chol., 587 mg sodium, 59 g carbo., 4 g fiber, 11 g pro.
Daily Values: 28% vit. A, 43% vit. C, 6% calcium, 20% iron
Exchanges: 1 Vegetable, 2 Starch, 2 Other Carbo., ½ Fat

Home Run Garlic Rolls

You'll score big when you serve these warm garlic-and-Parmesan-topped rolls to the hungry team.

Prep: 20 minutes   Rise: 30 minutes   Bake: 13 minutes   Oven: 350°F
Makes: 24 rolls (12 servings)

> 1 16-ounce loaf frozen white or whole wheat bread dough, thawed
> 1 tablespoon butter or margarine, melted
> ⅛ teaspoon garlic powder
> 2 tablespoons grated Parmesan cheese

1. Lightly grease a 13×9×2-inch baking pan; set aside. Shape dough into 24 balls. Place balls in prepared pan. Cover; let rise in a warm place until nearly double (about 30 minutes).

2. Bake in a 350° oven for 13 to 15 minutes or until golden. Meanwhile, in a small bowl combine melted butter and garlic powder. Brush butter mixture over hot rolls; sprinkle with Parmesan cheese. Serve warm.

Nutrition Facts per serving: 102 cal., 1 g total fat (1 g sat. fat), 3 mg chol., 26 mg sodium, 16 g carbo., 0 g fiber, 3 g pro.
Daily Values: 1% vit. A, 4% calcium
Exchanges: 1 Starch, ½ Fat

186

Victory Scoops

Personalize these frozen dessert treats by letting the kids choose their favorite yogurt flavor and coatings.

Prep: 20 minutes   Freeze: 30 minutes to 6 hours   Makes: 8 servings

> 1½ cups coarsely crushed frosted cornflakes
> ¼ cup chopped cocktail peanuts
> 2 tablespoons miniature candy-coated semisweet chocolate pieces or miniature semisweet chocolate pieces
> 8 scoops low-fat frozen yogurt or light ice cream (any flavor)

1. Line a baking sheet or tray with waxed paper; set aside.

2. In a shallow dish combine cornflakes, peanuts, and chocolate pieces. Roll scoops of frozen yogurt, one at a time, in cereal mixture, forming a ball and pressing cereal mixture onto sides. Place coated scoops on prepared baking sheet; cover with plastic wrap. Freeze up to 6 hours.

Nutrition Facts per serving: 167 cal., 5 g total fat (2 g sat. fat), 10 mg chol., 97 mg sodium, 26 g carbo., 1 g fiber, 4 g pro.
Daily Values: 10% vit. A, 6% vit. C, 31% calcium, 2% iron
Exchanges: ½ Starch, 1 Other Carbo., 1 Fat

Index

Note: Page references in **bold purple type** indicate photographs.

189

Metric Information

The charts on this page provide a guide for converting measurements from the U.S. customary system, which is used throughout this book, to the metric system.

PRODUCT DIFFERENCES

Most of the ingredients called for in the recipes in this book are available in most countries. However, some are known by different names. Here are some common American ingredients and their possible counterparts:

* Sugar (white) is granulated, fine granulated, or castor sugar.
* Powdered sugar is icing sugar.
* All-purpose flour is enriched, bleached or unbleached white household flour. When self-rising flour is used in place of all-purpose flour in a recipe that calls for leavening, omit the leavening agent (baking soda or baking powder) and salt.
* Light-colored corn syrup is golden syrup.
* Cornstarch is cornflour.
* Baking soda is bicarbonate of soda.
* Vanilla or vanilla extract is vanilla essence.
* Green, red, or yellow sweet peppers are capsicums or bell peppers.
* Golden raisins are sultanas.

VOLUME AND WEIGHT

The United States traditionally uses cup measures for liquid and solid ingredients. The chart below shows the approximate imperial and metric equivalents. If you are accustomed to weighing solid ingredients, the following approximate equivalents will be helpful.

* 1 cup butter, castor sugar, or rice = 8 ounces = ½ pound = 250 grams
* 1 cup flour = 4 ounces = ¼ pound = 125 grams
* 1 cup icing sugar = 5 ounces = 150 grams

Canadian and U.S. volume for a cup measure is 8 fluid ounces (237 ml), but the standard metric equivalent is 250 ml.

1 British imperial cup is 10 fluid ounces.

In Australia, 1 tablespoon equals 20 ml, and there are 4 teaspoons in the Australian tablespoon.

Spoon measures are used for smaller amounts of ingredients. Although the size of the tablespoon varies slightly in different countries, for practical purposes and for recipes in this book, a straight substitution is all that's necessary. Measurements made using cups or spoons always should be level unless stated otherwise.

COMMON WEIGHT RANGE REPLACEMENTS

Imperial / U.S.	Metric
½ ounce	15 g
1 ounce	25 g or 30 g
4 ounces (¼ pound)	115 g or 125 g
8 ounces (½ pound)	225 g or 250 g
16 ounces (1 pound)	450 g or 500 g
1¼ pounds	625 g
1½ pounds	750 g
2 pounds or 2¼ pounds	1,000 g or 1 Kg

OVEN TEMPERATURE EQUIVALENTS

Fahrenheit Setting	Celsius Setting*	Gas Setting
300°F	150°C	Gas Mark 2 (very low)
325°F	160°C	Gas Mark 3 (low)
350°F	180°C	Gas Mark 4 (moderate)
375°F	190°C	Gas Mark 5 (moderate)
400°F	200°C	Gas Mark 6 (hot)
425°F	220°C	Gas Mark 7 (hot)
450°F	230°C	Gas Mark 8 (very hot)
475°F	240°C	Gas Mark 9 (very hot)
500°F	260°C	Gas Mark 10 (extremely hot)
Broil	Broil	Grill

* Electric and gas ovens may be calibrated using celsius. However, for an electric oven, increase celsius setting 10 to 20 degrees when cooking above 160°C. For convection or forced air ovens (gas or electric) lower the temperature setting 25°F/10°C when cooking at all heat levels.

BAKING PAN SIZES

Imperial / U.S.	Metric
9×1½-inch round cake pan	22- or 23×4-cm (1.5 L)
9×1½-inch pie plate	22- or 23×4-cm (1 L)
8×8×2-inch square cake pan	20×5-cm (2 L)
9×9×2-inch square cake pan	22- or 23×4.5-cm (2.5 L)
11×7×1½-inch baking pan	28×17×4-cm (2 L)
2-quart rectangular baking pan	30×19×4.5-cm (3 L)
13×9×2-inch baking pan	34×22×4.5-cm (3.5 L)
15×10×1-inch jelly roll pan	40×25×2-cm
9×5×3-inch loaf pan	23×13×8-cm (2 L)
2-quart casserole	2 L

U.S. / STANDARD METRIC EQUIVALENTS

⅛ teaspoon	= 0.5 ml
¼ teaspoon	= 1 ml
½ teaspoon	= 2 ml
1 teaspoon	= 5 ml
1 tablespoon	= 15 ml
2 tablespoons	= 25 ml
¼ cup = 2 fluid ounces	= 50 ml
⅓ cup = 3 fluid ounces	= 75 ml
½ cup = 4 fluid ounces	= 125 ml
⅔ cup = 5 fluid ounces	= 150 ml
¾ cup = 6 fluid ounces	= 175 ml
1 cup = 8 fluid ounces	= 250 ml
2 cups = 1 pint	= 500 ml
1 quart	= 1 litre